Lindsay's Luck: A Fascinating Love Story

Frances Hodgson Burnett

Printing Statement:

Due to the very old age and scarcity of this book,
many of the pages may be hard to read due to the
blurring of the original text, possible missing pages,
missing text, dark backgrounds and other issues
beyond our control.

Because this is such an important and rare work, we
believe it is best to reproduce this book regardless of
its original condition.

Thank you for your understanding.

CONTENTS.

LINDSAY'S LUCK.

BY MRS. FRANCES HODGSON BURNETT.

AUTHOR OF

"KATHLEEN," "THEO," "PRETTY POLLY PEMBERTON,"
"MISS CRESPIGNEY," "A QUIET LIFE," ETC.

CHAPTER I.

BLUE BLOOD AND CALICO.

LADY LAURA TRESHAM had just come down stairs from her chamber to the break-fast parlor. I mention this, because at the Priory everything that the Lady Laura did, became a matter of interest. And why not? She was a visitor, she was a charming girl, she was Blanche Charnley's special friend and confidante, she was Mrs. Charnley's prime favorite; the Rector himself was fond of her; and all the most influen-

tial young members of the High Church at Guestwick (the Rev. Norman Charnley's church,) were
in love with her, and watched the maroon curtains of the Charnley pew far more attentively
than they watched the antique carven pulpit, of
which the Guestwick aristocracy were so justly
proud.

I have said Laura Tresham was a charming
girl, and I repeat it, adding my grounds for the
assertion.   Perhaps I can best do this by presenting her to my readers just as she stands before
the large, open Gothic window of the cosey, old-
fashioned little breakfast-room, the fresh morning
sunlight falling upon her, the swallows twittering
under the ivied eaves, — ivy gothic window and
sunlight forming exactly the right framing and
accompaniments to Lady Laura Tresham as a
picture.   She is just tall enough to be sometimes,
in a certain girlish way, thought regal; she is
just fair enough to be like a stately young lily;
she has thick, soft, yellow blonde hair; she has

blue, velvet eyes, and with her long, white morning dress, wears blue velvet trimmings just the
color of her eyes; for it is a fancy of hers to
affect velvets, because, she says, ribbons don't
suit her. But, in spite of this assertion, it really
would be a difficult matter to find anything which
did not suit Laura Tresham. Everything suits
her, or rather it is she who suits everything.
Blanche Charnley, who adores her, thinks there
is nothing like her beauty, and her stately, high-
bred ways. All that Laura says, or does, or
thinks, is, in Blanche's eyes, almost perfect, and
she will hear no other view of the matter expressed. In true girl-fashion, the two have vowed
eternal friendship, and they discuss their little
confidences together with profound secrecy and
the deepest interest.

Every summer Laura comes to the Priory for
a few weeks at least, and every winter Blanche
has spent in London for the last four years. The
Charnleys are irreproachable. The Reverend

Norman was a younger son, but fortune smiled
upon him, nevertheless. There is no richer living
than Guestwick in England or Wales, and certainly no more aristocratic one. The country
gentry and nobility attend the High Church and
approve of the Rector. The family drive to ser-
vice in a velvet-lined carriage, while Blanche and
Mrs. Charnley make their charity rounds in a
pony phaeton, whose ponies are miracles of value
in themselves. Accordingly, any astute reasoner
will observe at once that it is impossible for even
that most select of dragons, Lady Laura's guardian, who is something slow and heavy in Chancery, to object to his ward's intimacy with the
Guestwick Charnleys, as they are called.

So Lady Laura has been Blanche's companion
from her childhood, and now is more her friend
than ever. So she makes summer visits to the
Priory, and so we find her this summer morning
standing at the breakfast-room window, and listening with some interest to her host and hostess

as they discuss the contents of an American letter the Reverend Norman has just received by the morning's delivery.

"I have never seen him," the Rector was saying, "but if he is at all like his father, he is a generous, brave young fellow; perhaps a little unconventional in manner, but still a thorough-bred gentleman in every noblest sense of the word. I shall be glad to see him for more reasons than one, and I hope you will make him feel as much at home as possible, Alicia, and you also, Blanche, my dear."

Lady Laura turned toward the breakfast-table.

"Who is he, Mr. Charnley?" she asked. "I suppose I may inquire, as I am to meet him, and I want to know. You see Blanche and Mrs. Charnley have the advantage over me, in knowing the whole story. What did you say his name was?"

"Robert Lindsay," read Blanche aloud, glancing at the signature of the open epistle, 'Yours, sincerely.' Papa, let Laura see this letter. It is so odd, and yet so — manly, I should call it."

"Certainly, the letter is quite at Laura's disposal," answered the Rector, with a smile. "Read it, my dear. I admire its tone as much as Blanche does."

Lady Laura came to the table to take the letter, and, as she stood, glanced over it with some curiosity in her eyes. It was rather a singular letter, or at least it was a letter that expressed a great deal of character. It was frank, fearless, and unconstrained; honest, certainly, and by no means awkward in its tone. The writer evidently did not lack worldly experience, and was not short of a decent amount of self-esteem. Such men are not common anywhere, but they are an especial rarity among certain classes; and in this case, English reserve and dread of appearing offensive, gave way to American coolness and self-poise. It was something new to Laura Tresham, and she looked up from the closing sentence and dashing signature, "Very sincerely, Robert Lindsay," with a soft little laugh.

"It is an odd letter," she said. "I don't think I ever read anything like it before. Thank you, Mr. Charnley."

"I am under great obligations to the young man's father," said the Rector, as he refolded the letter: "and I can never hope to repay him otherwise than by taking his place toward his son so long as he remains in England. I suppose we shall see young Lindsay soon. He says his epistle would scarcely have time to precede him by a day."

Robert Lindsay was pretty liberally discussed, as the breakfast progressed. Events had preposessed Mrs. Charnley in his favor, and the honest assurance of his letter had pleased and amused Blanche; but Lady Laura was merely curious about the new arrival, and had not as yet decided whether to like him or not. She was not so prone to sudden admiration as Blanche,

and she had a secret fancy that this simple, frank
young fellow might become a trifle tiresome
through the very frankness of his simplicity.
She had also a decidedly English dread of any
freedom of manner, or tendency to the ignoring
of conventionalities, which is the popular idea
of an American in England; so she listened to
the conversation somewhat dubiously.

The day passed, as days generally did with the
Charnleys. They had a pleasant way of spend-
ing days at the Priory; so pleasant, indeed, that
people said killing time was the forte of the
family. No one ever felt the hours drag at that
establishment. Lady Laura was as fond of the
Priory as Blanche Charnley herself. "One could
be so deliciously idle there," she said, but she
did not add that after all, the idleness did not
imply loss of time. There was more company
at the Priory than anywhere else in the Shire;
and the young eligibles who watched the big,
ancient pews on Sundays, rode over from their

respective homes so frequently, that a day rarely
passed in which there was not quite a respectable
party out on the grounds, or in the delightful
old oak-paneled parlor, playing croquet, or stringing bows and handing arrows, or talking pleasant
nonsense to pretty Blanche Charnley, and making gallant speeches to her friend. Half a dozen
of them were there the day of the arrival of
the American letter, and among the rest came
Col. Treherne, who was blonde, aristocratic, long
limbed, and leonine in type. Blanche Charnley
had a quiet fancy that Laura did not dislike Col.
Treherne. Her manner to him bore better the
construction of cordiality than her manner toward
her numerous adorers usually did; sometimes it
seemed even tinged with a certain degree of
interest, and once or twice, when she had ridden
out with her groom, she had returned with Col.
Treherne at her side, and a bright, soft color on
her fair face. But Blanche was not partial to
Col. Treherne. She did not like his air of calm

superiority; she did not like his regular patrician features and fair skin; she objected even to his long, fair mustache, and his favorite habit of twisting it with his white hand; and she absolutely detested the reflective coolness of the questioning glance that generally accompanied the action, when he was annoyed or wished to repress any approach at familiarity. But of course, she was very polite to Col. Treherne when he came to the Priory. She was too thoroughbred, in spite of her energetic likes and dislikes, to exhibit either openly; so she merely confined herself to the few stray shots good breeding admitted, in the shape of an occasional polite little sarcasm, or a quiet move against her aversion's game.

This particular evening, as she stood with the little party on the archery-ground, watching the gentleman stringing her friend's pretty satinwood bow, and handing her arrows, she felt her dislike even more strongly than usual. There was a spice of romance in Blanche Charnley's gay nature, and her love for Laura Tresham was touched with it. She had a cherished fancy that the man who won such a gift must be perfect of his kind. He must be brave and generous, and whole-souled in every chivalrous sense. He must reverence the woman he loved beyond all else, and he must value her love as the great gift of God to man. There were to be no half measures in its depth, no shade of self-worship, no touch of weakness; he must be ready to wait, to do, to dare for her pure sake. He must

"Love one maiden only, cleave to her,
And worship her by years of noble deeds,
Until he won her."

Geoffrey Treherne was not that man. His love for Lady Laura was only a pleasant sacrifice upon the altar of his lofty self-consciousness. He was a well-bred individual, and, in a certain punctilious fashion, scrupulously, haughtily honorable; but he would not have "fallen down and wor-

shiped." In his own way he cared for Laura
Tresham. Her fair face, and proud repose of
manner, pleased him; the adoration she exacted
pleased him. The woman he married must be
capable of exciting admiration. Her name was
as ancient a one as his own; although he felt
that she was worthy of the honor he intended
doing her. Naturally, it was not all calculation,
though probably calculation predominated. He
was a man, after all, and he loved her, and was
ready to sue for her favor, after his own fashion;
but he was not Blanche Charnley's ideal of a
lover for her friend.

So, with the consciousness of this on her mind,
Blanche Charnley felt dreadfully out of patience,
as she listened to Laura's clear, soft-toned voice,
and noticed that she seemed by no means dis-
pleased. Once or twice she even thought she
saw her blush faintly, at some of her companion's
speeches; and Lady Laura was not prone to
blushes, and, to Blanche's quickened senses, the

soft touch of color appeared suspicious. Suppose
she really cared for him? And then, why should
she not? The world would call the match a suit-
able one, in every sense of the term. In the
depth of her momentary vexation, Blanche dropped the arrow she held in her hand, and bent to
pick it up, before the gentleman who stood by
her side had time to see it.

"Dear me!" she sighed, unconscicusly. "I
wish somebody respectable would come — anybody, so that it wasn't Geoffrey Treherne."

"I ask pardon," said her escort. "I really
did not understand what you said, Miss Charnley."

She looked up and laughed.

"Oh, excuse me!" she said. "I was thinking aloud, I believe. How very rude! It is I
who should ask pardon." But in her anxiety she
brought some diplomacy to bear against the
enemy during the remainder of the evening.
She gave him no opportunity to improve upon
any advance he might have made, and played

2

" third party " so effectually, that Treherne actually found himself at a loss, in the face of his dignified self-consciousness, and accepted the Rector's invitation to dinner in sheer self-defence.

Half an hour after the other visitors had made their adieux, and the two young ladies had gone to their respective rooms, Lady Laura, who was sitting under the hands of her maid, heard a loud summons at the hall-door, and, when the summons had been answered, the sound of voices.

She raised her head with something 'of curiosity.

" I did not know Mr. Charnley expected visitors, Buxton," she said, to her waiting-woman.

Buxton, whose hands were full of the shining, yellow, blonde tresses, did not know that visitors were expected either. " Unless it might be the American gentleman, my lady. Mrs. Charnley said it was possible he might come earlier than they had expected."

" Oh, yes! " said Lady Laura, indifferently.

The American. I have no doubt it is. I had forgotten."

Buxton had not completed her task, when a little rap at the door announced Blanche Charnley, who, being a quick dresser, had completed her toilet early, and now entered, eager and bright, in her pretty, fresh dinner costume. She came and seated herself at the toilet-table at once, looking even more animated than was usual with her.

"Papa's visitor has arrived, Laura," she said. "I was on my way down stairs when he made his appearance, and I had an excellent view of him."

"Indeed!" returned her friend. "And the result?"

Blanche nodded her head prettily.

"An excellent one, my dear," she answered, laughing a little. "Robert Lindsay will 'do.' He is stalwart, he is dark, he is well-featured, he is even handsome, and I know he is a desirable individual. He is not the least bit like Col. Treherne, Laura," meditatively. "And he carried his own valise."

"My dear Blanche!" exclaimed Lady Laura, raising her eyes in no slight astonishment.

Blanche laughed, and nodded again.

"Absolutely did," she said. "And the effect was not an unpleasant one, despite its novelty. He carried it well, and looked quite at ease, and honestly pleased, when he held it in one hand and gave the other to papa, who came out into the hall to meet him. I really don't believe Geoffrey Treherne would have looked so thorough-bred under the circumstances."

Lady Laura did not make any reply, but the suggestion was scarcely a pleasant one to her mind. The idea of Col. Treherne carrying his portable baggage in his faultlessly-gloved hand, was such a novel one, that it appeared almost absurd. That gentleman's valet was the envy of all his acquaintance, from the fact of his intense respectability and desirable repose of manner, and Col. Treherne would decidedly have disapproved of any campaign which would not have admitted of his attendant's presence.

Blanche was evidently prepossessed in the new visitor's favor. She chattered about him with good-humored gayety, and described his appearance to her listener with less of disposition to satirize than she commonly displayed. The novelty of a gentleman who carried his own valise, had pleased her; and the fact that the gentleman in question was not at all like Geoffrey Treherne, had pleased her still more.

At last Buxton had finished, and Lady Laura rose and stood before the swinging mirror to favor the satisfactory result with an indolent glance of inspection.

"What a lovely creature you are, Laura," said Blanche, with a little laugh. "That soft, pale-blue dressing-gown makes you look like a blonde angel. What is it Tennyson says,

"A daughter of the gods, divinely tall,
And most divinely fair."

There must be some satisfaction in *your* looking at the mirror. All Buxton's art couldn't make my poor little fair head look such an aureole. Mr. Lindsay is quite dark, so I suppose he will at once fulfill the decrees of fate, by following Col. Treherne's august example."

"How absurd!" said Lady Laura, coloring faintly, however. "Blanche, I beg — "

But Blanche only laughed again.

"Why should it be absurd?" she asked. "He is a gentleman, after all, whether his father sold bales of calico or not. Do you know, Laura, I like these trading people. They are astute and thoroughbred often, and I believe in Ralph's favorite theory, that we poor representatives of the 'blue blood' are falling from grace. Now, really, why should not Robert Lindsay love you, and why should not you love Robert Lindsay, if he is worthy of it? Dear me, how delightfully astounded Col. Treherne would be."

It is scarcely necessary to record Lady Laura's reply. That young lady was astute also, and sufficiently so to conceal her quiet little predilections, even from her friend. Blanche's jest annoyed her a little, though she was far too wise to exhibit her annoyance; so she simply smiled, with a slight touch of reserve, and colored a little again, and then adroitly changed the subject.

CHAPTER II.

MIDNIGHT CONFESSIONS.

WHILE Lady Laura's toilet was being completed, after Blanche had gone down
stairs again, she gave the new arrival some slight
mental consideration, which, I regret to say, was
not so favorable as he really deserved it should
have been.   Was he really going to be intrusive?
Surely, something in his manner must have sug-
gested Blanche's jesting speech, absurd as it was.
Perhaps there was a tinge of Geoffrey Treherne's
haughty self-security in the object of Geoffrey
Treherne's admiration.   Lady Laura Tresham,
with her fair face, and her womanhood, and her
rent-roll, had the birthright to such a pride, and
but one or two persons who were fond of her
knew that, notwithstanding this, Lady Laura
Tresham was only a very pretty, very tender

very innocent girl, of whom experience would make the sweetest of women. Almost unconsciously to herself, Robert Lindsay was in her thoughts, as she went from her room across the broad upper landing leading to the stair-case, but still she was by no means prepared for a little incident chance brought about.

She had just paused for a moment to arrange the sweeping train of her dress before going down, when a door opened behind her, and the individual who came out, in his momentary embarrassment at finding her so near, trod upon the shining, purple silk before he saw it. It is quite possible that this occurred because he had seen Lady Laura first, and that, after his first glance at the aureole of crêpé yellow hair, and the delicate face slightly turned over her shoulder, he forgot the great probability of there being a lustrous yard-long train in her wake.

"I really beg pardon," he said the next instant. "Pray, excuse me, Lady Laura," and he colored to his handsome brown forehead.

The glance of the eyes upraised in reply, augmented his confusion. The young lady did not color not even ever so slightly, but she looked somewhat astonished. Her only reply was a calm, sweeping bow, and the next moment the silken purple train was rustling down the staircase, and the gentleman, who was no less than Robert Lindsay himself, remained standing upon the landing watching its progress with the most unconscious of honest admiration. Now this really was not a strictly conventional mode of proceeding; but, as I have before intimated, Robert Lindsay was not a strictly conventional individual. He was an honest, handsome, fearless young fellow, and his honest beauty and fearlessness were his chief characteristics. Chance had thrown him into a somewhat novel position, but it was a position whose novelty he was too thoroughly manly to feel embarrassed under. He had been glad to meet his host, and he had honestly endeavored to repress his inclination

toward any antagonism for the august but frigid
Treherne. He had thought Blanche Charnley a
delightfully pretty girl, and now as he stood at
the head of the stair-case and watched Lady
Laura Tresham's sweeping purple train and fair-
faced golden head, he forgot that it was unusual
for gentlemen to exhibit an admiration in so
deliberate a fashion, and remaining stationary,
decided that he had never seen a woman so
lovely, so fresh, so delicate, and so well dressed,
in the whole course of his existence.

There was a curious little excitement upon
him, brought about by the unexpectedness of
the encounter, and this little excitement made
him turn into his bed-room again, before going
down after the train had disappeared; and taking
his stand before an open window, he waited a
few minutes for the fresh night air to cool him
off.

"It would have been a pleasant sort of thing,"
he said, almost unconsciously; "a pleasant sort

of thing, if a man had lived in olden times, to have ridden to battle with her little glove in one's helmet.   In that rich purple, it looked like a lily — her hand.   Golden hair, too, bright and shining — just such hair as fellows like Tennyson rave about.   I wonder if Treherne — Pah! No. I forgot she did not know me when I called her Lady Laura.   Laura!   Perhaps Petrarch's Laura was such a Laura."

When he went down to the drawing-room, he found Treherne bending graciously over Lady Laura's chair, the velvet, blue eyes, softly downcast as he talked.   The most prejudiced individual could not fail to acknowledge that Geoffrey Treherne was a handsome man, even in his least prepossessing moods; and now, having in some sort recovered from his temporary disappointment in his deferential graciousness, he was really very courtly-looking indeed.   Still, Robert Lindsay did not show to any disadvantage as he bowed low before Lady Laura, when Mr. Charnley pre-

sented him. His tall, stalwart figure had a self-
asserting strength that Treherne's lacked; his
clear-cut, brown face, and clear, straight-glanced
eyes, were as perfect in their beauty as a man's
might be, and the natural ease and fearlessness
of any self committal in his manner to Blanche
Charnley's mind, at least, was worthy of admiration. But Lady Laura, not being prone to enthu-
siasm, saw only as she rose slightly from her
chair, a very tall, rather good-looking individual,
who had caused her some little surprise a few
minutes before in addressing her familiarly by
her name, and who was, at the present time,
rather tending to increase it by the unconcealed
admiration of his glance. It was evidently an
admiration not easy to conceal, and it expressed
itself unavoidably, as it were, in the frank, brown
eyes even once or twice after Mr. Robert Lindsay
had taken his seat at the dining-table, exactly
opposite Lady Laura Tresham. How could he
help it? Every time he looked up, he saw the

pure girlish face, with its softly, downcast eyes, the delicate, bare, shadowed throat, and the aureole of bright, crêpé hair; and, in spite of himself, the honest delight he experienced, portrayed itself, to some extent, in his countenance.

The Reverend Norman being a generous, hospitable gentleman, was very much predisposed in his young guest's favor. Really Robert Lindsay was apt to prepossess people through the sheer power of his great physical beauty; and, again, his was one of the rare cases, in which there can be no diminution of favorable opinion. He was a good talker, through right of a sweet voice, a clear brain, and a quick sense of the fitness of things. He had traveled as much as most men, and had seen more. He had enjoyed his youth heartily, and appeared likely to enjoy his manhood; and, at twenty-six, despite a pretty thorough knowledge of the world, he still retained a simple chivalrous faith in things good and true, such as few men can thank Heaven for the possession of.

Occasionally, during the evening, Lady Laura found herself regarding him with some interest. There was a novelty in this fearless man that impressed her, and attracted her attention. He was talking to Blanche about a hunting trip he had made in California, when her eyes were first drawn toward him. It was a wild, adventurous story he was telling; but he was plainly telling it well, and with such a man's hearty, zestful remembrance of its pleasures; and Blanche was listening, her look of amused interest not unmixed with a little admiration. He had not been intrusive so far, notwithstanding his frank eyes, and the trifling singularity of conduct in his watching her passage down stairs; accordingly Lady Laura felt herself at liberty to judge him impartially. He was handsome, certainly; and a certain air of boyish freshness and spirit in his style, was whimsically pleasant. How he seemed to be enjoying the jests he was making, and how well his gay laugh chimed with the ring of

Blanche's. He would be a very hearty, honest lover for some woman one day, and then, unconsciously, she glanced up at Geoffrey Treherne, who stood at her side, holding her little lace fan.

"Our friend seems to be enjoying himself," said that gentleman, with calm disapproval of the new arrival's being so thoroughly at his ease. Col. Treherne felt, in an undefined manner, that the young man ought to be a little overpowered under the circumstances.

But, singularly enough, whatever the cause of the phenomenon might have been, Lady Laura did not respond so cordially as her companion had expected. In fact, her manner was rather coldly indifferent, when, after glancing across the room, she made her reply.

"I had scarcely observed," she said. "Blanche appears to be interested, however, and Blanche is usually not easily pleased. Mr. Lindsay is a very pleasant sort of person, I should judge."

Treherne's hand went up to his big, fair mustache, doubtfully. He did not understand this. He felt as though he had been slightly repressed, and he liked Mr. Robert Lindsay none the better for it, for, little as that "pleasant sort of person" was to blame, he could not avoid connecting him, in some indefinite manner, with the polite rebuff he had met. Surely Lady Laura did not intend to countenance this person by even the mildest of lady-like championship. He turned around and looked down at her; but the lights of the glittering, pendant chandelier shone down upon the most tranquil and untranslatable of fair faces, and he was fain to smooth his mustache again, and decide, mentally, that this was an excessively unsatisfactory state of affairs.

It was late when the family retired, but it was not too late for Blanche's customary visit to her friend's chamber. During Lady Laura's stay at the Priory, few nights passed without pleasant, girl-like chats being held in one apartment or the other. Blanche's dressing-room adjoined

8

Laura's, and, upon this occasion, her young ladyship had just dismissed her waiting-woman, when
the young lady made her appearance in dressing-
robe and slippers, brush in hand, her abundant,
pretty, fair hair hanging loosely about her.

"I want to have a long chat to-night, Laura,"
she said, after she had tucked her small, slippered
feet under her gay wrapper, on the most luxu-
rious little lounge in the room. "You are not
tired, are you? You don't look tired. The fact
is, you never do look tired. How delightfully
flossy and yellow your hair is; you are sitting in
an actual bower of gold. I always think my
hair is pretty until I look at yours. Now, tell
me what you think of Robert Lindsay?"

All this, in one gay, little rattling speech,
sounded exactly like Blanche Charnley, and no-
body else; and then she shook her fair tresses
back, and paused for a reply, with something
more watchful in her eyes than one would have
imagined the careless question warranted.

"Now 'i is to be an honest opinion, Laura," she added, "without the least regard for the bales of calico, and entirely unbiased by any stately remembrance of that first august Tresham, who came over with the Conqueror. What —do—you—really—think—of—Robert Lindsay?"

"Think?" said Lady Laura, complacently, and with some slight, young lady-like mendacity, be it known. "I think he is very big, my dear; and really, I believe, that is all I have thought just yet."

Blanche's pretty shoulders were shrugged expressively.

"That is so like you, Laura," she said. "And it is exactly what I expected, too. I knew you wouldn't do him justice, poor fellow. Well, suppose I give you *my* opinion of Mr. Robert Lindsay. I—think—he—is—splendid!"

Lady Laura drew a long, shining, heavy tress over the white arm, from which the open sleeve of the blue dressing-robe fell back, and she looked at the shining tress, and the white arm approvingly, as well she might.

"Why?" she asked, concisely.

"Because he is honest," said Blanche. "Because he believes in things; because he is manly and chivalrous. Do you know, Laura, he was honest enough to tell me that you were the loveliest woman he had ever seen; and he said it as gravely and reverently as if he had been speaking of his own mother."

Lady Laura flushed even to her white forehead.

"You are either talking nonsense, Blanche," she said, "or I can tell you something else that I think of Mr. Lindsay."

"What else?" asked Blanche.

"That he is very insolent," was the reply.

Blanche merely laughed and shrugged her shoulders again, with a comical little grimace, as she answered this rather intolerant speech.

"I don't think he is," she said, practically. "I wish he had said it of me; or I wish somebody else had said it, with the proviso that they had said it just as he did. He was speaking the truth, and one hears so many white fibs in these days, that the truth is as astounding as it is refreshing."

But she did not refer to Robert Lindsay again that night. Perhaps she thought she had said enough; at any rate, during the rest of their conversation, his name did not once occur; and when she rose from her lounge at last, to go to her room, they had wandered so far from Robert Lindsay that such an individual might never have had existence

CHAPTER III.

ROSES AND THORNS.

BEFORE many days had passed, Lady Laura found room for more than temporary interest or temporary annoyance. She found room for a surprise, which became in a short space of time something like amazement. She would have thought very little of Mr. Charnley's guest after the first evening of their meeting, had she not found herself compelled to think of him through the agency of a rather unexpected fact, which forced herself upon her notice. This young man of whom, gentleman as he was, in her calm, intolerant pride she had thought little more than of one of her guardian's lackeys; this young man, whose father was a tradesman, and whose grandfather, she had heard Mr. Charnley say, was an excellent farmer; this young

man was, in the most unprecedentedly matter-
of-fact manner, falling into the same position
as Geoffrey Treherne himself. She could not
understand how it had come about, and far less
could she avoid it; she could only begin, as time
progressed, to feel that it was so. It would have
been the most impossible of tasks to repulse him.
His genial, hearty nature was not easily chilled;
and even Treherne found his frigid stateliness
met with a careless gayety that perfectly overwhelmed him. Lindsay's honest, undisguised admiration showed itself in every action, and Lady
Laura found herself sheerly helpless against him.
It was useless to endeavor to chill him: clearly
he was determined to persevere, in sublime disre-
gard of the fact that Geoffrey Treherne and
William the Conqueror stood between him and
the object of his admiration. He cared little for
Geoffrey Treherne, it seemed, and less for William
of Normandy; and yet, in spite of his persistence, he was never intrusive. And, notwith-

standing her astonishment, Laura Tresham could
not resist wholly a slight inclination to feel interested in him in some degree. If it had been
easier to dislike him, she would have felt herself
in a safer position, but to dislike him was a sheer
impossibility. She had tried the iciest reserve,
and he had waited patiently, until she was compelled to thaw into at least a reasonable warmth;
and this being the result of her efforts, good
breeding afforded her no alternative; and yet
she was not quite prepared for the somewhat
remarkable sentiment to which the gentleman
gave utterance upon one occasion.

They were sitting together in Mr. Charnley's
study, one evening, when the conversation turned
incidentally upon a certain *mesalliance* that was
the subject of great discussion among the aristocratic dragons of Guestwick, and which had
caused said dragons much severe contempt and
disapproval, and Mrs. Charnley was echoing the
public sentiment, though, of course, more chari-

tably than was usual with the dragons, when Rob
Lindsay (people always called him Bob, he said),
spoke up, with a not unbecoming earnestness of
belief in what he was saying.

"I don't think I agree with you, Mrs. Charnley," he said. When a man loves a woman honestly, he forgets everything but that he does love
her honestly. He does not think so much of her
superiority or inferiority as he does of the fact
that he loves her. The woman I marry, were
she queen or empress, will be to me simply the
woman who is dearest to me on earth."

Mrs. Charnley smiled, but Blanche, who had
been teasing her macaw, as it swung in its gilded
cage over the window-plants, turned round and
gave him a long, keen, quiet glance, as if while
measuring his strength, she found the result satisfactory. Rob Lindsay had advanced in her good
opinion every day, though she rarely mentioned
him to Laura. A very short experience had convinced her that if cool, deliberate determination

was of any avail, Rob Lindsay needed no championship, and was surer of success than most men.

Lady Laura herself did not vouchsafe him a glance. When he spoke, she was taking a book from the library shelves; and when, after a few minutes she replaced it, there was a faint glow of unwilling color on her cheeks. And later that very evening she had cause for still greater and more indignant bewilderment.

She had been out in the morning, making calls with Blanche, and upon her return had accidentally left one of her gloves upon a table, in the parlor. About an hour after the discussion in the library, she remembered the mislaid article, and went to the room to look for it, and as she entered her eyes fell upon the stalwart, good-looking figure of Rob Lindsay, who was standing in the middle of the apartment, with his back turned toward her. He did not hear her entrance, and at first she scarcely comprehended his pre-occupation ; but the next instant, a glance at the pier-glass opposite to him revealed to her the true state of affairs. He held her lost glove in his hand, and was regarding it as it lay upon his palm with a great deal of quiet admiration, and before she had time to speak, he had complacently put it into his vest-pocket. He saw her the moment after, and turned toward her with a coolness and freedom from embarrassment that completely overpowered her, and rendered her helpless, notwithstanding her indignation. He must unavoidably have known that the mirror had reflected everything to her, and yet he was as placidly self-contained as would have been possible under any circumstances.

"I actually did not hear you come into the room," he said, with audacious cheerfulness.

His coolness so staggered her, that for an instant she only looked at him haughtily.

"I left one of my gloves here, this morning, Mr. Lindsay," she said at last, "and I came to find it. It was on this table, near Blanche's card-case, I believe. It was a mauve glove, with white silk tassels;" and she looked at him with steady scrutiny that should have abashed him, but which to her astonishment failed to do so.

He turned to the table, as cheerfully as ever, without a shadow of discomposure in his manner.

"It doesn't appear to be here now," he said. "A mauve glove, you said, with white, silk tassels. I believe I remember noticing it, this morning, as being a very pretty glove. It would be a pity to lose it."

Lady Laura did not waste time in any further search. The ends of the identical white silk tassels were at that moment showing themselves above the edge of the pocket of his vest, and he had not even the grace to blush, while he was perfectly conscious of the fact that her eyes were resting upon this final touch of strong circumstantial evidence.

On her way to her room, Blanche met her upon the stair-case.

"Where have you been, Laura?" she asked. "Your eyes look positively dangerous! What is the matter?"

"Nothing," said the young lady, briefly. "I have been looking for my glove, and — and — I haven't found it. Don't keep Mr. Lindsay waiting, Blanche. I shall not have time to join you at present, and you know he promised to give you another archery lesson."

Blanche ran down stairs, with a glimmer of suppressed fun in her eyes, and, when she reached the bottom of the stair-case, she found Robert Lindsay at the hall-door, looking out upon the lawn with a most untranslatable smile. It was a calm smile, and a baffling one, and not at all an unsatisfied smile, in its way; and it was on the cheerful, handsome face, even after half an hour spent in the archery-ground. Then, after making several very bad aims at the target, Blanche set another arrow, and drew her bow with most delicate precision

"And so Laura couldn't find her glove, **Mr.** Lindsay," she said.

Mr. Lindsay looked with great complacency first at the aim his pupil was taking, and then at his pupil's pretty face.

"Why, no!" he said, regretfully. "I believe she did not. And it was a pity, too, you know, because it was such a very pretty glove. A little mauve affair, with white silk tassels, and a delicious, little, delicate dead ghost of a perfume about it."

"Yes," admitted Miss Charnley, sagaciously. "I know the glove. Laura always does wear pretty gloves, and — There, Mr. Lindsay," as the little, white-winged arrow whizzed away. "Right in the centre of the target."

"In the very centre," replied the immovable Rob. "And it is what I should call a very excellent aim too, Miss Blanche."

For the next day or so Mr. Rob Lindsay encountered some rather rough sailing, if so indefinite a term may be employed. In Laura Tresham's creed, presumption was the sin unpardonable; and Robert Lindsay had been guilty of an act of presumption, which had no equal in her experience. If he had shown the slightest shadow of embarrassment, or the slightest touch of penitential regret, she might have found it possible to vouchsafe him a haughty pardon; but as it was, his immovable composure baffled her terribly. As far as was possible, without causing remark, she had held herself aloof from him, scarcely deigning him a word or glance; but it had not produced the effect she desired. He did not intrude himself upon her, but he certainly did not avoid her. He was as gay and good-humored as ever, and seemed to enjoy himself as thoroughly. The Reverend Norman was very fond of him, and with Mrs. Charnley he was as great a favorite as Lady Laura. In his good nature, his good spirits, his boyish daring, and his almost affectionate warmth of manner, were combined all the most desirable characteristics of a favorite son ; and Mrs. Charnley, with true motherly recollection of the Ralph of whom Blanche had spoken, and who was the only son of the house of Charnley, regarded this brave, high-spirited, dashing young fellow, with something of a motherly affection. Accordingly, she wondered somewhat at Lady Laura's cold reception of her eulogistic speeches, but Blanche understood the matter pretty clearly. Laura no longer avoided mentioning Rob Lindsay. In their nightly discussions she spoke of him with cutting sarcasms. She laughed at him, and sneered with extraordinary aptness at his unconventional frankness and warmth of manner ; and certainly poor Rob had never met with more severity than he sometimes met with in the bright little dressing-room. Still he seemed to sustain himself through it all with wonderful cheerfulness. Even when he had been most cuttingly satirized, and when his pleasant speeches

were received with the most frigid hauteur, he
appeared to make himself most thoroughly comfortable. He drove the little pony-carriage for
Mrs. Charnley when she wanted to make her
charitable rounds; he arranged her foot-stool for
her when she was tired; he had ridden over to
Guestwick and matched Berlin wools for Blanche
to a shade; he had rendered himself popular
with every one, and even the dullest, longest
days were made cheerful by his indefatigable
good-humor. Taking all this into consideration,
it is easy to see that Lady Laura's task was a
difficult one. It was difficult to satirize him to
Blanche as mercilessly as she felt inclined; and,
of course, it was impossible to satirize him openly.
And besides, it appeared quite probable that even
under such circumstances, he would have encountered the satire as he encountered every other
weapon. So she found herself compelled, much
against her will, to submit to the sheer force of
circumstances.

4

After the advent of the new arrival, Col. Treherne's visits became even more frequent than they had been before. Perhaps, notwithstanding his self-consciouness, he had been quicksighted enough to see a dangerous rival in a man who was generous, imperturbable, and physically beautiful in no slight degree, in grand defiance of his lack of pedigree. Women were subject to whimsical fancies after all, and even such a woman as Laura Tresham, with all her inborn prejudice and pride, might be influenced by such a man's persistence, if persistent he should presume to be. And in her secret resentment against Rob, Laura was more cordial in her reception of Treherne's advances than she would otherwise have been. She was more chary of her smiles, less inclined to reserve, and altogether more encouraging. But Geoffrey Treherne simply regarded this as the very natural result of his attentions. It was, of course, not likely, after all, that any rival should be successful against him, when it came to action; and yet, notwith-standing his certainty upon the subject, he felt more at ease when he found that his influence did not appear to be at all lessened, and in his security he forgot something of his hauteur, and was more condescendingly familiar in his manner toward the object of his former distaste.

"This American seems to be a gentlemanly sort of young fellow," he said, graciously, one day to Blanche. "Not highly polished, of course, but good-natured enough, at all events, I think."

It so happened that this morning he had called earlier than usual, and had found Blanche and her friend in the garden, with Rob, who was giving them the benefit of his floral experience; and Blanche in gloves and a neat little garden-blouse, was trimming one or two of her favorite rose-bushes with a pair of keen little scissors. She was snipping away the dead leaves in a most scientific manner, when her companion vouch-safed this condescending patronage of her favor-

ite; and she went on snipping like a very charming picture of unconscious innocence, as she
made her reply.

"Now do you really, Col. Treherne?" she said.
"How very kind in you to say so. This is a
pretty rose, isn't it? And how delighted—"
Snip, snip, snip—"Mr. Lindsay would be if I
were to tell him. Don't you think so?"

Treherne looked down at her with reflective
uneasiness. Her pretty little straw hat hid her
bent face from him, and the scissors in the small
gloved hands were very busy; but he was by no
means a dullard, in spite of his arrogance, and
he felt an uncomfortable sense of the fact that
Miss Blanche Charnley was satirizing him rather
cuttingly, and added to this, was an equally
unpleasant consciousness that he had made himself slightly ridiculous.

"Pray, excuse me," he began stiffly. "I was
not aware that my words could contain any
offence."

"Oh, dear, no!" replied Blanche, with much delightful simplicity. "Of course not. How could they? You see these sort of people are not like we are. I dare say it is very likely that they don't sneer at *our* pretensions. And of course, Mr. Lindsay ought to be much obliged to you for your good opinion; and if he wasn't, it would be very ungrateful on his part. But then do you know, Col. Treherne, I really don't believe, taking all things into consideration, that I would patronize him more than was absolutely unavoidable. It might interfere with his natural feeling of deference, you see."

It was rather severe upon Treherne; perhaps, a little too severe, upon the whole; but Blanche Charnley was apt to be severe, occasionally; and she had been wondering for some time if a quiet, suggestive lesson might not prove beneficial. Her sense of the ridiculous made her keenly alive to Geoffrey Treherne's peculiarities, and besides, she was a little out of patience with

Laura; so she went on to her next rose-bush in the significant silence that followed, with a quiet consciousness of the fact that she had at least made a telling shot.

There was a sort of uneasiness in Treherne's manner during the remainder of his visit. He did not like Blanche Charnley very much, but he had a true English horror of making himself absurd; and the idea of having appeared absurd to Robert Lindsay, was particularly distasteful to him. Satirical as Blanche's speech had been, it had suddenly presented a new idea to his mind. Was it possible that this young fellow was quicker sighted than his careless gayety had led him to imagine? Once or twice he had fancied that he detected a thread of Blanche Charnley's keen-edge sarcasm in his quietly daring speeches.

These thoughts were very busy in his mind, when, the young ladies having gone to change their gardening dresses, he found himself promenading one of the terraces with the cause of his late annoyance.

CHAPTER IV.

THE DEBATABLE GIFT.

TREHERNE and Lindsay had been walking to and fro for some minutes in silence, but at length it was broken by Lindsay himself.

"I have some excellent 'weeds' in my pocket, Treherne," he said. "Allow me to offer you one. I brought them from Cuba myself."

It was a very pretty bead-embroidered cigar-case that he produced, and the cigar Geoffrey Treherne accepted was the rarest and most fragrant of its kind; but he scarcely looked at either cigar-case or cigar, after his first word of thanks; his eyes had fallen upon something Lindsay had drawn from his pocket accidentally, and which had dropped upon the terrace near one of the young man's shapely feet; a very small article after all, but it had attracted Treherne's attention in one instant. It was a pretty mauve glove with white silk tassels.

The next minute Lindsay saw it too, and stooped to pick it up with the most collected of quiet faces.

" I think I have seen that glove before," said Treherne, stiffly, " or am I mistaken ? "

" Why, no," returned Rob, good-humoredly. " I don't think you are mistaken. It is quite possible you have seen it before, I dare say. Won't you have a light ? "

With the utmost composure, he had returned it to his pocket, and brought out a box of fuses, and having handed them to his companion he stopped his walk for a moment, to light his own cigar.

" I imagined I had seen Lady Laura wearing it," said Treherne, helplessly. He was in a fever of impatience, and could scarcely govern himself.

" Possibly," said Rob, puffing. " The fact is,

it did belong to Lady Laura," with intermediate puffs.

"Then you are a very fortunate individual," commented Treherne, frigidly.

Rob took his cigar from his mouth, looked at its glowing end for a moment, and then tossed his spent fuse away, looking as undiscomfited as ever, which was really very trying to his companion.

"No," he said at last, "I can't say that I am very fortunate, Treherne; sometimes I am almost inclined to think that I am rather unfortunate. Of course, Lady Laura did not give me her glove; and, of course, I am not such a vaunting idiot as to pretend that she did. Neither am I such an idiot as to imagine that she would have given it to me if I had asked her. I found the glove and I kept it. It is a pretty glove, and the woman I love has worn it, and, though it may not be a great loss to her, it is a great gain to me. I like to carry it about with me, and look at it sometimes, and that is how it fell from my pocket. I should not have mentioned it if you had not seen it; and I should not have mentioned it, if I had not wished it to be impossible for you to misunderstand Laura Tresham. Good cigars, these, ain't they?"

Treherne's reply was a somewhat incoherent one. In fact he had never been so utterly taken aback in his life. There was a coolness about this young man's manner, that was altogether too much for him. Treherne was determined to sift the matter as early as possible, and in his anxiety to sift it, he did a rather unwise thing. When Lady Laura came back again, he found himself alone with her for a moment; he brought the conversation somewhat abruptly to bear upon the subject most important to his ease of mind.

"This Japanese lily is a great favorite of Blanche's," said Lady Laura, tranquilly, as she bent over a flower; "and Mr. Lindsay says — "

"Our eccentric friend seams to be a great

favorite,' interposed Treherne, in his secret anxiety. "I wonder if you are aware that he
carries one of your gloves in his pocket, Lady
Laura ?"

A sudden pink flush flooded Lady Laura's bent
face in an instant, even touching the light waves
of hair upon the white, low brow, and sweeping
over the slender throat. Her confusion was so
evident that Treherne found himself becoming
slightly confused also, and feeling more awkward
than he had anticipated, and accordingly his next
speech was an unfortunate one.

"He was good enough to explain to me," he
said, " that you had no knowledge of the fact of
his having it in his possession. He had found
the glove, he said, and kept it."

Lady Laura interrupted him, a curious little
tremor stirring the folds of muslin over her neck,
a curious, dangerous glow in her eyes.

"I ask pardon, Col. Treherne," she said; "but
may I inquire if you really felt it was necessary

to catechise Mr. Lindsay concerning the manner
of his obtaining possession of my glove?"

Treherne was dumbfounded. For some reason
appearing inexplicable to him, the young lady
was evidently annoyed in no slight measure.
He did not understand that the very pride he
had admired as mating so well with his own, had
arrayed itself against him.

"I am bound to say," he explained loftily,
" that there was no necessity for so doing. Mr.
Lindsay was honest enough to be desirous of
making sure that there could be no misunder-
standing."

"He was very kind," replied Lady Laura,
now feeling inconsistently severe against the
delinquent. "Very kind, indeed; but he was
mistaken in saying I did not know he had the
glove. I saw him take it." With that she
turned away.

Through his intense discomfiture, Col. Treherne
left the Priory earlier than was customary with

him; and it was after he had gone, that Rob
Lindsay, sauntering into the drawing-room, found
Lady Laura there, and was addressed by that
young lady in a very decided manner.

"I am glad you are here, Mr. Lindsay," she
said to him. "I have just been wishing to see
you. Col. Treherne tells me that you found the
glove I lost, and — and that, in fact, you showed
it to him a short time ago." This last artful
touch as punishment beforehand.

For the first time in the course of her acquaintance with Mr. Rob Lindsay, Lady Laura had the
pleasure of seeing him blush. The color ran up
to the roots of his curly-brown hair; but it was
not a blush of embarrassment. It was clearly a
flush of high, uncontrollable indignation.

He walked deliberately to the bay-window.

"I ask pardon, Lady Laura," he said, with
startling warmth. "But may I ask if Col. Treherne said that I had exhibited your glove to
him?"

The sudden change from his usual careless gayety to this somewhat foreboding frankness of demeanor frightened her fair young ladyship, in spite of herself. She actually felt herself on the brink of being most ignominiously defea' d, and Rob Lindsay, waiting for a reply, saw the blue-velvet eyes that matched the blue-velvet ribbons, change their expression curiously.

"No," faltered the young lady. "He merely said that — that he had seen it."

Rob s knitted forehead smoothed slightly.

"Oh!" he said, more coolly. That is a different matter, you see. I am rather glad to hear it, too, because if it had been otherwise, I should have been compelled to say that Col. Treherne had not adhered strictly to the truth. I did *not* show Col. Treherne your glove, Lady Laura. It dropped out of my pocket accidentally, and he saw it, and I — Well, I spoke the truth about it."

He had never looked better in his life than he

did when he finished saying this, and leaned against the side of the bay-window, looking down at her with a spark of the fire which had not quite died out in his brown eyes. He saw that he had startled her a little, and, despite his smouldering wrath, he was tenderly sorry for it. He was not the man to feel he had frightened a woman ever so slightly by any thoughtless warmth of speech, without a chivalrous regret.

"You must excuse my seeming abruptness, Lady Laura," he said, in his good-natured, frank fashion. "I misunderstood you at first, and if Treherne had really given you the impression that I had boasted of my luck in finding the glove, he would have given you a false impression, and one which must necessarily have made me appear contemptible in your eyes, and I could not stand that, you know."

"I cannot understand," said Lady Laura, her attempt at making a strong point a terrible failure. "I really cannot understand why you took the glove in the first place. It was very absurd, and you must know that — that it made me appear very absurd, too."

"Absurd!" said Rob. "In whose eyes, Lady Laura?"

"In my own," she faltered, coloring until she looked like one of Blanche's pink verbenas. "In Col. Treherne's, and — and in yours." This last with great weakness.

"Not in mine," said Rob, exhibiting great cheerfulness. "Don't say that, if you please."

"But I mean it," returned Laura, breaking off a rose geranium-leaf, and trying to regain her coldness of manner. "You have made me feel absurd, at least, to have placed me in a very annoying position, Mr. Lindsay. Why, it is impossible for me to understand."

Rob looked down again for a moment, with a meditative air, at the averted face, and the white hand toying nervously with the geranium-leaf, and then he turned his eyes away toward the garden, and, forgetting himself for the time being, first whistled softly, and then stopped.

"Ah! Why, indeed!" he said.

Having crushed the perfume out of one leaf, Lady Laura threw it away, and took another, and began again, utterly ignoring both whistle and exclamation.

"Having subjected me to this annoyance, you subject me to still another," she said, "the annoyance of asking you to return the glove to me."

Rob's countenance fell somewhat.

"I am sorry that I have subjected you to any annoyance," he said, with honest penitence. "Very sorry, Lady Laura; but I believe I am quite as sorry to hear you say you want your glove again. Of course, you don't care for any reasons I may have for wishing to keep it. It is a little thing to you, and you can afford to ignore it as you do, but —"

"I was not aware that I ignored anything," interposed Laura, inconsistently.

5

Rob went on calmly.

"But I can assure you it is a matter of more importance to me. But that doesn't matter, does it?"

He stopped here, and drew the glove from his pocket; but he did not offer it to her at once. He held it in his hand, and looked at it a little regretfully and sadly.

"A very little thing to ask for," he said. "And a very little thing to prize, it might seem; but I prize it, nevertheless. A very little thing to be refused, too — is it not, after all? But as I suppose Treherne has a greater right to it than I, why, here it is, Lady Laura;" and he laid it upon the little work-table of Blanche's, which stood between them, therein exhibiting more discretion and diplomacy than one would have expected of so frank a young man.

I have already spoken of this unconventional Rob's great physical beauty, and of the effect it was apt to produce in the way of softening peo-

ple's hearts toward him; so you will not be
surprised at being told Laura Tresham was softened a little. This momentary look of regretful-
ness was very becoming to him withal, and he
had been straightforward and regardful for her,
at least. And then a half-worn glove was such a
little thing, and then — Well, she looked up at
his handsome brown face, and his handsome
brown eyes, and relented somewhat. Besides,
had he not intimated that his rival had a right,
which that rival had not?

So the glove lay untouched upon the table.

"Col. Treherne has no right to it," she said,
with some degree of hauteur. "He has no right
that you or any other friend of mine has not."

"Friend?" was Rob's quiet echo.

"I believe I said friend," she answered.

But she did not attempt to take the glove, and,
when a few minutes later, Blanche called to her
from the garden, she turned to obey the summons as though she had forgotten it; and when

Rob drew her attention to it, she paused a moment, hesitating.

"It is of no value to me," she said, carelessly, at length. "I don't know where its fellow is, and I should not wear it if I did. If you wish to keep it, you may, since perhaps that will prove to you that no one has a right to dispose of it but myself."

Rob took the glove in his hand, swinging it lightly by its silken tassels, his comely face brightening.

"Thank you," he said. "I do want it, and I suppose the speech I am going to make is rather an audacious one, but I can scarcely help making it, notwithstanding. The fact is, Lady Laura, l should not like to feel that the annoyance I have caused you has forced from you the gift I value so highly."

"It is certainly not a matter of compulsion," she said briefly. "You wished to have the glove, and I gave it to you."

"Thank you again," answered Rob, all the cheerfulness in the world expressing itself in his composure of manner.

And as Lady Laura left the room, the mauve glove, for which Geoffrey Treherne would have given something very considerable, was quietly replaced in the pocket from which, to Geoffrey Treherne's blank amazement, it had dropped a few hours before.

CHAPTER V.

NEW ARRIVALS.

WITH true feminine inconsistency, almost before she had reached Blanche, Lady Laura had repented her impulse of generosity somewhat. Notwithstanding the malicious turn of Fortune's wheel against him, Geoffrey Treherne had by no means wholly lost his power over her, and her inward conjectures as to what his exact opinions would be if he knew the truth, made her feel slightly conscience-stricken. She could not altogether resist the idea that if chance should reveal to him this little incident as it had revealed to him the other, the result would be the very natural one of some slight embarrassment being entailed upon her, notwithstanding the fact that she had left him to draw his own conclusions on the subject but a short time before.

But then she had been very securely innocent,
and now — was she? Was she as securely innocent, regarding Mr. Lindsay himself? Had she
been very secure when she had looked up at his
honest, indignant face with that little guilty thrill
of fear and admiration? She had tried to believe
at the time that it was only a thrill of surprise,
having its foundation in the sudden knowledge
that this immovable person could flash into such
becoming wrath; but it did not require many
moments' consideration to force upon her that it
was a guilty thrill, and had held its own unpleasant significance. She remembered, too, un-
willingly, times when Robert Lindsay's straightforward speeches, and practical, frank ways, had
given her somewhat of the same thrill before;
and when, by contrast with other men she knew,
and had in some sort admired a little, he had
seemed worthy of any woman's respect and
friendship; yes, even worthy of the love of any
woman who was endowed with a woman's natural

love of fearlessness and honesty. But then it would never do to encourage Robert Lindsay, nevertheless. The fact is, that, stately as she was in her girlish way, Lady Laura Tresham was a terrible beautiful coward, and in her mind there was a very natural awe of the weighty individual who was something stupendous in Chancery. She had stood in awe of this gentleman from the first hour of her wardship, and even now, in her young ladyhood, she was as much afraid of him as ever. She had heard him discourse with stupendous solidity of eloquence upon William the Conqueror, and the barriers of society, and the stately obligations under which the unfortunate descendants of William the Conqueror and his court had been placed by those august personages having condescended to be born, and live, and " come over " and establish a somewhat intrusive authority over unborn generations. Lady Laura's guardian held as a religious creed, to be religiously sustained, that the circumstance of a stately-bearing Norman noble, having been called Basil de Tresham, entailed upon this blue, velvet-eyed, golden-haired young lady, descended from him, the necessity of being solidly majestic also; and that all this blue, velvet-eyed, golden-haired young lady's little secret, tender prejudices, must be crushed under the brazen idol of her name's antiquity. So, with her guardian and the brazen idol constantly before her as models, it is no wonder that Lady Laura had innocently fallen into a groove of opinion not unlike them, unless in its being softened and made prettier by the fanciful form it adopted. But, nevertheless, she had been rather tired of William of Normandy, and Basil de Tresham, sometimes. Now and then her guardian had tired her, and now and then she had been tired of his aristocratic eligibles, when they appeared (as they not unfrequently did) in the form of languid dandies, who wore faultless dress-coats, and neck-ties, and gloves, and parted their hair in the middle, and were loftily conscious of their families belonging to the peerage, and their rent-rolls representing themselves through the medium of a respectable row of figures. But she had never been tired of Rob Lindsay. The young man had a very simple way of accounting for himself, and was very practically straightforward in his assertions that he had nothing to boast of in the matter of pedigree.

"You see," he had said, on their first discussion of the subject, "it cannot possibly matter to one now, as I understand it, whether the founder of the family (that's what you call it, isn't it?) was an illustrious individual or a plowman who bought his bread and cheese with sixpence a day. The family was founded, you know, and the man's dead, and this generation has arrived at — Robert Lindsay; and with Robert Lindsay lies the rest, honor or dishonor. And it really seems to me, Mrs. Charnley, and

Miss Blanche, that the settling of such a question rightly has nobility enough in it, without
troubling oneself about a man who has moul-
dered centuries ago, and who was not to be
blamed or praised for either the sixpence or the
bread and cheese, or on the other hand, for the
series of lucky accidents that made him a baron.
Many as good a man as the first Plantagenet
followed the plow till the day of his death, who
would have been as great as Geoffrey, if he had
found the same chance."

Thus had Mr. Robert Lindsay expressed himself, and thus had Lady Laura heard him, with
a sense of recognizing a fresh and not unpleasant
novelty in the speech, despite its rank heresy.
Still it is not to be supposed that even such
honest observations as these could overcome the
prejudices of a lifetime at once. But they had
impressed Lady Laura through all her girlish
pride in name and birth; and this day her
remembrance of them made her feel like a young

lady who had been self-convicted of heresy and
falseness to the inherited creed of her forefathers.

So, feeling after this manner she repented her
generosity, and as the tide of her thoughts
turned, blamed Rob Lindsay for both generosity
and repentance, which was unjust, to say the
least of it. She made up her mind during the
day's uneasiness that followed, that from this
time forward Mr. Robert Lindsay must really be
effectually checked. Accordingly, she applied
herself to the task of checking him, and stood
upon guard with great vigilance. Perhaps Rob
was somewhat surprised; perhaps, being prone
to deeper thought than society in general imagined, the result was not so great a surprise to
him as might have been expected. But, as it is
customary with story-tellers to reveal to the public the private soliloquies of the principal char-
acters, whether plotters or plotted against, who
play parts in their stories, I will record a simple
soliloquy of my hero's, which arose from the
occurrence of several untoward events.

It was about a week from the morning of the interview in the bay-window, when, during one evening, Col. Treherne having called, Col. Treherne's star had seemed very plainly in the ascendant, and Rob, upon retiring for the night, had, perhaps, felt a thought depressed, in spite of his usual elasticity of spirit. He had not advanced at all, and fate had been so far against him that he had, for the first time, felt himself at some slight disadvantage among the little party of Treherne's friends, who had followed that gentleman's august example in paying visits to the Priory, and addressing the Rev. Norman's household goddesses. They were polished, good-natured men, upon the whole, and by no means dullards in any sense; they had every advantage of wealth and pedigree, and William the Conqueror had done his best for them, so that not Basil de Tresham himself could have caviled at their antecedents; and, cheerful as he usually was, Rob had felt this a little; and he had felt also with a faint, natural sting, that the best natured of them felt, however unconsciously and good-naturedly, that this stranger was scarcely of themselves. But he had borne up against it well, and his genial gayety had engendered an unusual feeling of friendliness and cordiality toward him, which, together with Blanche's thoroughbred tactfulness, had saved him from what might have been a greater bitterness; and when he went to his room, he was not, after all, as discomposed as a less cheerful, well-natured individual might have been. Then it was that he gave utterance to the soliloquy which I regard it as my privilege to record. He had paced the floor with some degree of restlessness at first, but he had cooled off at length, and brightening a little, he stopped, and taking the mauve glove, from its hiding-place, kissed it.

"Fate goes against a man sometimes," he said, with renewed courage of tone; "but what is worth winning is worth waiting for. If your

hand was in it, Laura — " kissing the glove
again. "But, as it is not, I suppose I may as
well console myself with the fact that I have the
glove, and Treherne has not — which is one step
forward, at least."

And in the bright, cozy little dressing-room,
only a few yards away, another step forward was
being taken, in which he had no share.

With a girl's quick instinct, Laura had observed
his slight discomfiture, and had dwelt upon it,
as it might be, as a means of self-defence. It
would be less difficult to be strong against a man
who was at a disadvantage, than against a man
who was popular, high-spirited, and successful.
For a little flash of triumph, for which she
secretly despised herself, she had been incautious
enough to bring the conversation to bear upon
the subject, in hopes that Blanche might unconsciously second her ; but the result of her manœu-
vre was by no means a favorable one.

"It seems really unaccountable to me, Laura,"

said Blanche, "that you dislike Mr. Lindsay so. I am sure he is very nice, and I am sure he likes you. I don't agree with you in the least, either, about his being awkward; and I thought he never appeared to a greater advantage than he did this evening, when 'the odds were against him,' as Ralph would say."

Laura elevated her lovely eyebrows.

"Of course, 'the odds' were against him," Blanche went on. "One couldn't help seeing that, and seeing, too, that he felt it a little. But which of the men that were here this evening would have sustained themselves as coolly under the circumstances? Did you see how good-humoredly he put down that detestable little Vicars, when he pretended to have forgotten his name? It reminded me of Lion patronizing Ralph's terrier. The Honorable little Eustace will never snub him again, you may depend upon that, my dear."

For private reasons of her own, Laura forbore

to make any comment upon the subject. This was certainly not encouraging to a young lady who had determined to regard Mr. Lindsay in a ridiculous light. Woman naturally favor the stronger party; and Rob Lindsay so often showed himself the stronger party, through virtue of his peculiar coolness of demeanor. He had shown himself the stronger party when he had made his composed reply to the little honorable, which reply had so successfully nonplused that small scion of a noble house, and caused him to be covered with confusion as with a garment. He was showing himself the stronger party now, since Blanche Charnley had been enlisted in his favor with her whole battery of satirical speeches. Lady Laura changed the subject.

"Didn't I hear Mr. Charnley say something about the probability of your brother returning shortly?" she asked, for the simple reason that she had nothing more apropos to say.

"Yes," answered Blanche. "I forgot to tell

you, by-the-by. Papa had a letter from him this morning. He says we may expect him in a day or two. I was glad to hear it, for I was afraid he would not be here in time to see Robert Lindsay; and I know Ralph will like Robert Lindsay."

Laura subsided into silence in despair. Robert Lindsay again! Was it impossible to avoid Robert Lindsay under any circumstances?

Blanche did not remain in the room as long as usual that night. After her last speech, Laura was not inclined to be very communicative, so, after a few minutes' vain endeavor to rouse her to her customary animation, Blanche rose to go, and coming behind the chair on which the graceful, blue-robed figure sat, she lifted a mass of the pretty bright amber hair in her hands, and, after holding it for a moment in an affectionate, caressing, thoughtful fashion, she bent over and kissed her friend's smooth, carmine-tinted cheek.

" Good-night!" she said, in a manner lighter than her pretty action had been, " and pleasant

dreams! Ah! my fair, careless goddess, what a
charming thing it would be if you were only not
my Lady Laura Tresham."

A few days later Ralph Charnley returned
from Oxford, and, through his arrival, fortune
worked very industriously against Robert Lindsay. Ralph Charnley was a gay, dashing, astute
young fellow, noticeable chiefly for a wonderful
exuberance of spirits. He was a popular man,
withal, among the country-side aristocracy; and
his return was the signal for a fresh influx of
company, and a new stock of amusements. There
came picnics in the Guestwick woods, evening
parties, excursions to the little neighboring sea-
port town for moonlight sails; and, in the general
bustle of gayety and confusion, Rob Lindsay
found himself separated quite as effectually from
the object of his admiration by a single dignified
dowager, or a pretty, chattering girl, as he could
have been by the Atlantic Ocean itself. As
Blanche had predicted, Ralph conceived a won-

derful fancy for him, and before a week had passed they were almost inseparable. Ralph had a true English love of sport, and Rob, with his remembrance of wild adventure, had a great power of fascination in his less experienced eyes. His sporting seasons had comprised more than a few day-shots, fired in roaming over a preserve with an attendant game-keeper in the rear, and iced wines and game pies waiting somewhere in the shade. He had lain by his camp-fire through long starlit nights, and hunted through long days of an excitement not without its peril. He had killed as much game in two months as the highly respectable keepers of the Guestwick preserves could have killed in two years, even though the Guestwick preserves were considered something quite worth boasting about. Thus Ralph Charnley's interest increased daily, and was finally not unmixed with admiration.

"He is a first-rate fellow, that Lindsay," he said to Blanche, one evening. "What a favorite he would be at such a place as Oxford or Cambridge, where men find their level. We had just such a fellow at Oxford once — a Scotchman; and he was the most popular man there. Just such a fellow as Lindsay, and had lived just the same life, I suppose; and he could ride, and shoot, and fence like the deuce. I ask pardon, Lady Laura. It is odd, too, how gentle such men generally are. You don't find such magnanimity and tenderness in men with insignificant muscles. Douglas — that was the Scotchman's name — had a little sister — a tiny, deformed creature, with a wasted body, and big, seraphic eyes; and he used to wait on her like a woman. Some of the men had been to his mother's house, and they said that when the child was in one of her paroxysms of pain, no one could touch her but Douglas; and when she died, she died in his arms. That is one reason why I say Lindsay is like him. It appears there is just such another pitiful little creature in one of the cottages near here, and the under gardener tells me that Lindsay has taken a fancy to her; goes to see her almost every day; and the child fairly lives in his visits. I believe he is there now."

"He never mentioned it to us," said Blanche. "I wonder how it was?"

"Oh! he is not likely to mention it!" said Ralph. "He isn't that sort of fellow, you see. Men of his kind are not apt to talk about what they do. If I were a woman, I would trust my life to such a man as Lindsay without a copper farthing, rather than to trust it to William the Conqueror himself."

Necessarily, this was rather an aggravation of her wrongs, to the young lady, who sat at a little distance, diligently endeavoring to concentrate her attention upon the little basket of gay flosses and wools on her knee. Her small pearl-pink ears were gradually warming until she almost fancied that their glow must be perceptible. If this state of affairs lasted much longer, it would be useless to contend against the tide of public opinion.

If she had given her secret inclination the rein at that moment, forgetting Basil de Tresham and the awe-inspiring Chancellor, Lindsay's chance of success would have been a very good one. But that was not so easy as might appear, to the uninitiated. Of course she did not love Robert Lindsay as yet, and, really, she was secretly very much afraid of her guardian. And then Geoffrey Treherne? If Geoffrey Treherne had been less eligible, or the Chancellor less pompously imposing, Ralph Charnley's words would have turned the tide wondrously that bright, autumn morning. But, as it was, she did not love Robert Lindsay yet. So she was saying, mentally. She was safe yet, and might she not make herself safer still by saying yes to the momentous question which Geoffrey Treherne had asked her the night before. She was almost desperate enough to be driven to do so, even while she had scarcely decided as yet that Geoffrey Treherne was more to her than Robert Lindsay.

The Charnleys had arranged for the next day, one of the jolly, unique little excursions for which they were so justly celebrated. It was to be a shooting party, and, after the gentlemen had spent the earlier part of the morning on the moors, they were to repair to a place of rendez-vous, where the ladies and luncheon would await them. Then it was that Geoffrey Treherne was to be answered, in consideration of some nervous hesitation on Laura's part the preceding evening. Nothing was clearer than that the gentleman was not fearful of failure. It could scarcely be otherwise than that he should be successful; and this tranquil belief his manner had plainly demonstrated.

Lady Laura scarcely regarded the excursion with any degree of pleasurable anticipation. The truth was, she had some slight dread of it.

Perhaps she was a little afraid of her august lover, or, at least, sufficiently so, to make a negative somewhat d.fficult to pronounce. It was so evident that he expected a "yes" that it would not be by any means an easy matter to surprise him with a "no."

"I have actually no choice left," she exclaimed, unconsciously, with pathetic helplessness. "Oh, dear! what shall I do?"

Ralph had just left the room, and Blanche was reading, consequently the perfect stillness was broken by the sound of her voice.

"No choice about what?" asked Blanche, surprisedly, dropping her book. "What have you no choice about, Laura?"

"Only some wools," was the diplomatic reply. "I can't decide which to choose, rose or blue. I don't think I shall work any more. I am losing patience."

CHAPTER VI.

THE BETROTHAL RING.

TO every one but Lady Laura the shooting party was a perfect success. The weather was cool and bright, the spirits of all in most excellent order; the feminine portion conscious of appearing to great advantage; the masculine half conscious of being in the best of humors, and highly satisfied with the prospect before them. All the morning the report of numerous guns sounded over the moor-lands, and the purple heather-bells had been stained a deeper color as the little, fluttering victims fell; for, as it was the first of September, the slaughter of the innocents was to be ushered in with *eclat*.

At twelve o'clock the Charnley carriage had set down at the place of rendezvous its cargo of half-a-dozen pretty girls, and almost as many delicate little hampers; and Col. Treherne's respectful and respectable man-servant, with an assistant, was moving respectfully here and there, drawing forth from inexhaustible corners, wonderful compact arrangements for the further development of a delicate, compact luncheon, so called. Said luncheon was in a temptingly complete state when the report of the guns began to sound nearer, and then ceased; and soon the shooting party made their appearance, followed by the attendant game-keeper, hungry, elated, and not by any means in reduced spirits.

Behold Geoffrey Treherne, in a faultless, velvet shooting-costume of Lincoln green; behold Ralph Charnley, in a brown one; behold divers other eligibles, in divers other faultless costumes, and last, but not least, Robert Lindsay, surpassing himself in the matter of good looks, and wonderfully surpassing the rest, with the aid of shooting costume, and his muscular, well-knit figure and comely face.

Lady Laura, standing a little apart, under a huge oak tree, and looking particularly girlish and lovely, as she persistently worked her parasol into the moss at the tree's root, glanced up as the sportsmen approached, and favored them, comprehensively, with a bow. It was not intended for Treherne, individually, and it was certainly not intended for Rob Lindsay; but both gentlemen acknowledged it markedly—Treherne with a gratified composure of manner, and Rob with a slight, deferential raising of his hat from the crisp, brown, close curls. From the general interest displayed by the party, it was very evident that, in some sort, Mr. Robert Lindsay had distinguished himself in the public opinion. There was much cordial commendation of his prowess, and much deferring to his modestly expressed opinion on sporting subjects, over the luncheon. The Honorable little Eustace had plainly changed his mind about patronizing the big, good-humored young fellow; and, amid the

popping of champagne corks, Mr. Rob Lindsay
became, after a mild fashion, a retiring Nim-
rodian hero.

"He was the best shot among us, Lady Laura,"
eulogized Ralph Charnley, who was taking his
luncheon with unconventional ease, on the sward
at that young lady's feet. "And some of the
fellows were pretty good shots, too. I wish you
could have seen the way he brought down a
pheasant Treherne missed."

"I thought Col. Treherne was an old sports-
man," said Laura, with meditative annoyance.

"So he is," answered Ralph. "But he is not
up to Lindsay. The fact is, Lady Laura, Lindsay
is one of a thousand, in my opinion. He is a
living proof of my theory that a man can exist
without a great great-grandfather. See what a
splendid fellow he is; look at his physique, and
then compare him with that little snob Vicars.
And I really am not sure whether the founder
of the Vicars family was not William of Nor-

mandy himself, or William of Normandy's aunt. Men like Lindsay, strong, fearless, quick-witted fellows, are what the world wants in these days; and they are more sparsely scattered than they should be, though, if one is to judge of him, they are plenty enough in America, where people grow more fresh and vigorous than they seem to grow here."

Thus through nearly half the hour spent round the luncheon, and then, as she loitered over her plate, Lady Laura was favored with another expression of the public opinion, coming from a sturdy game-keeper, in drab leggings, who stood a few paces from her, talking to Treherne's man-servant.

"He bean't no fool, that American chap," sagaciously commented he of the leggings. "They can't none on 'em beat him, I tell you, my lad. No bangin' away and hittin' nowt fur him. What he bangs at is bound to coom down. An he's a fine, hearty-natured young chap, too —

cheerful like, an' pleasant i' his ways. It's him as is so kindly to that little, weakly thing o' Jarvis's."

Then it was that, under the accumulation of her trials, Laura Tresham came to a desperate resolve. What that resolve was may be easily guessed by what followed as a result. When Geoffrey Treherne took the place Ralph Charnley had vacated, she received him with great steadiness of demeanor. It could scarcely be said that her manner was encouraging, as far as any cordiality might be concerned, for it really was not; still it was not actually discouraging; and from that time until the party separated, the gentleman scarcely left her side, and was so composedly assiduous in his attentions, indeed, that his air had almost a tender authority in it. As for Lady Laura herself, she really appeared to be in a singular mood. She looked a little excited, and, once or twice, a false note strangely shook the usual even sweetness of her voice. Above all other things, Blanche Charnley noticed that she persistently avoided Robert Lindsay. She even diplomatized a little to avoid encountering him when they reached the Priory, and immediately after tea was over, she went to her room upon plea of indisposition.

It was about two hours later that Blanche, following her up stairs, and going to her chamber, found her sitting there alone, with an open book in her hand. She was not reading, however, and scarcely appeared to have been doing so. The light of the tapers upon the dressing-table, showed two bright pink spots glowing in her cheeks, and a curious, heavy, suspicious glitter in her eyes.

When Blanche entered, she half closed the book, suddenly, with her forefinger, however, between the pages. She had not retired, she explained, because her head had ached too badly, and now it was better, and she had been reading.

There was a new anxiety in Blanche's mind,

is she took a seat upon the lounge near her friend. Geoffrey Treherne's tender assiduity had held its own significance to her, and she was anxious to sift the truth to the bottom. But as, of course, it would not do to approach the subject at once, she chattered away with her usual animation, and let the conversation take its own turn; and at last it drifted, as if by chance, to Geoffrey Treherne himself, and, finally, upon a ring Geoffrey Treherne had that day worn.

It was a singular affair, this ring; a single, great, flashing diamond, set like a crystal teardrop upon the merest slender thread of gold. It had belonged to the Trehernes since the first Treherne had set it upon the betrothal-finger of the first English bride of their house; and from generation to generation it had been handed down as betrothal-ring for scores of fair brides. There was a sort of superstition attached to it, Blanche said. Those who wore it were bound with a magic tie to their liege lords, and no

7

woman could ever be freed from the spell, who had worn it if only for an hour.

But as she related her legend, Blanche observed that the pink spots on Laura's cheeks glowed deeper until they had almost deepened to scarlet. She was somewhat uneasy, it seemed, even at first, under the recital; but when the last touch of superstitious belief was added, the scarlet suddenly faded, and the book she had lightly held slipped away from her detaining finger, and fell upon the carpet at her feet. She stooped to pick it up instantly; but as she raised it, Blanche suddenly uttered an exclamation, and, catching her hand, held it up to the light of the waxen tapers.

"Laura!" she exclaimed, actual tears of despair and disappointment starting to her eyes. "Oh, Laura! what have you done?" For there, upon the slender forefinger, glittered the flashing diamond, imprisoned by the slender thread of gold — the Treherne diamond, that had held so many Treherne brides to their faith by the power of its magic spell.

"Tell me the truth," demanded Blanche. "It doesn't mean—Laura, it can't mean—" And there she stopped.

Lady Laura drew her hand away, not blushing, as a young lady might have been expected to do under the circumstances. Indeed, if the truth must be told, she looked slightly impatient, in spite of her little, nervous laugh.

"Yes, it does 'mean' Blanche," she said. "It means that the spell is upon me, too. It means that I am engaged to Geoffrey Treherne."

CHAPTER VII.

SHE SHALL NOT MARRY HIM.

THE ominous gold-imprisoned crystal had flashed upon Laura Tresham's finger for some short time, when a slow, new doubt gradually unfolded itself to her mental vision. Of course, in these days Geoffrey Treherne's visits had become an established custom, attended with less ceremony than they had formerly been, and of course, the members of the household understood their portent. In his triumph over his rival, Geoffrey Treherne had been in a manner loftily gracious. He could afford to be gracious now, and, perhaps, some slight pity for Lindsay rendered him more gracious than he would have been otherwise.

Naturally it could not be otherwise, than that, upon the first knowledge of the truth, Robert

Lindsay was, for the time, dashed and overcome.
He had scarcely expected such ill-fortune, at the
worst, and since it was unanticipated, it was all
the harder to bear. The first day he was somewhat more silent than usual, and his cheerfulness
of spirit seemed to have forsaken him; but the
second day he brightened up a little, and having
spent the third out upon the moorlands, shooting
with Ralph, he returned in the evening with a
well-laden game pouch, and, to all appearance, a
fresh stock of spirits. From that time he did
not alter his manner toward Lady Laura in the
least. He was as unvaryingly good-humored as
ever, and as cheerfully unmoved by any coldness
or avoidance on her part. Even Blanche, with
all her penetration, was puzzled. He might have
been acting in accordance with some steady,
purposeful resolution.

In the first flush of her fancied security, Lady
Laura convinced herself that her position was
not an unpleasant one after all. True, she had

pledged herself, and must, at some not-too-far
away period, fulfill her pledge; but then she was
safe; and just at this critical time safety was a
very desirable object to be attained.

But this was just at first. The excitement
worn away somewhat, she did not feel quite so
easy — she did not even feel quite so sure of her
safety; and, before two weeks had passed, once
or twice an occasional unpleasant secret fear had
forced itself upon her — the fear that "perhaps
she had made her throw rashly, and staked a
good deal for a safety not so secure as she had
imagined it would prove.

Coming in from the garden one day, she stopped in a little conservatory, opening into one of
the parlors, and, as she paused to examine a
newly-opened flower, she saw through the glass
doors that Blanche Charnley and Robert Lindsay
were in the adjoining room together, and she
caught the sound of the following comprehensive
sentence, deliberately enunciated, as though in

continuation of some before-expressed opinion by the gentleman.

"And when a woman, through any foolish fancy, or misguided pride, sacrifices herself to the wretchedness of marrying a man she does not love, her life will be a bitter wreck of all she has hoped for. And, on the honor of a gentleman, Miss Blanche, I believe that the man who might save her from such misery, and does not dare the risk, is not only unstable and weak of purpose, but is unworthy of his manhood."

Laura waited to hear no more. She had heard quite enough to prove to her that certain suspicions she had felt were by no means without foundation, and she hurried away. Here was a daring lover indeed! What reasons had he for supposing she did not love Geoffrey Treherne as a woman should love the man she marries? She had certainly not been demonstrative in her manner toward him; but then she never was very demonstrative, and she had tried very hard ·

not to appear cold. Robert Lindsay was insolent, presuming, audacious; but then how was
she to withstand his audacity? It seemed impossible. She had exhausted all her feminine
resources of coldness and hauteur, and this was
the result. Was ever young lady in such a strait
before? — absolutely in danger of being overcome in spite of herself, by a quietly-persistent,
cheerful lover, who most incomprehensibly refused to be rebuffed, refused to be overwhelmed,
refused to submit to circumstances, and insisted
upon retaining his spirits, and enjoying himself
in the face of everything! She was so influenced
by her adverse fate, that, during the remainder
of the day, she was incomprehensible also. She
looked uneasy; she lost her beautiful composure
of manner; she was actually a little cross to
Blanche, and she treated Rob Lindsay worse than
she had ever treated him before.

Running into Lady Laura's room accidentally
while she was dressing, Blanche found her frien

in tears, and was surprised to find her sympa-
thetic advances rejected somewhat unamiably.

"Please don't pity me, Blanche," she said,
with most unaccountable tartness. "I don't
want to be pitied, my dear. I have got the headache, and I am cross and out of humor with
everybody."

Blanche left her without expressing any further sympathy, and, going down stairs again,
innocently revealed the state of affairs to Rob
Lindsay, of course, without expectation of his
drawing any conclusions from the revelation.

"I found Laura crying a little just now," she
said. "She says she has the headache, and is
cross, which last statement may be entirely relied
on as being correct. What singular creatures
we girls are? I actually never knew Laura
could lose her temper until lately. Since the
shooting picnic she has been as nicely unangelic
as I should wish to see any one — as nicely unangelic as the rest of us. Geoffrey Treherne is
developing her resources."

The result of this communication was, that when Lady Laura came down, Rob met her with a very good-natured inquiry concerning her ailment.

"I was sorry to hear you were not well," he said, tranquilly. "Miss Blanche told me just now that you had the headache."

Lady Laura's blue, velvet eyes widened with some degree of haughtiness, and a tiny point of fire sparkled in them, suggestively.

"You must be mistaken," she answered, "or Blanche misunderstood me. I never had the headache in my life," which encouraging speech was made for the simple purpose of contradicting him, and making him feel uncomfortable.

But he did not look uncomfortable. He only smiled as tranquilly as he had spoken.

"I don't think I am mistaken," he said. "So, perhaps, it is possible that Miss Blanche misunderstood you. I am glad to hear that such is 'he case, for I thought you must be suffering

severely; in fact, she said you were crying!"
And he fixed his brown eyes on hers, the lids of
which were slightly heavy, and a little tinged
with faint pink.

That night Blanche Charnley was very fully
satisfied upon the subject of her friend's resources
having been developed. There was more warmth
under the fair, tranquil face, it appeared, than
people generally imagined. I think it probable
that every woman is spiced with a dash of hidden
fire, though it may only be developed upon rare
occasions; and the fire flashed forth brilliantly.
She was angry with Blanche for revealing her
secret irritation, angry with Robert Lindsay for
daring to listen, angry with herself for being
angry, and, in consequence, more irritable than
ever.

"It was ridiculous in you to tell him, Blanche,"
she said. "And it was insolent, on his part, to
mention it to me. I never disliked any one in
my life as I dislike that great, absurd giant of an

American; and I never saw any one so absurdly presuming, and awkward, and tactless, and under-bred!"

Her little flash of wrath cooled off after this, and then, of course, she began to regret her vehemence, and felt a little ashamed of herself, and, after that, nothing was more natural and girl-like, than to be a little low-spirited, and a little petulant; and at last, in the end, to burst into a flood of tears, in a fashion most unaccountable to every one but herself.

"I know it is foolish," she said. "And I know you think it is foolish, Blanche, but I am so — so miserable." And it was very evident that she was speaking the truth, however extraordinary such a truth might seem.

"Miserable!" echoed Blanche. "Miserable with that on your finger, Laura?" And she touched the Treherne diamond.

In this moment of her weakness, Laura forgot to be cautious, and forgot that she was talking to a very penetrating young lady. She flung out her hand with a petulant gesture.

"I hate it!" she exclaimed; and then suddenly recollecting herself, and regretting her dreadfully weak candor, she added, "At least I don't hate it; but sometimes I almost wish — I mean to say, I almost wonder if — if it would not have been better to have waited a little."

This diminuendo, together with her evident confusion, was very expressive.

"Ah, I dare say!" said Blanche, consolingly. "I thought so, from the first, Laura; but it is too late now."

Yes, it was too late now, very much too late, if the Treherne annals were to be relied upon; and this conviction, perhaps, made Laura Tresham more impatient than anything else would have. Before her engagement she had at least liked Geoffrey Treherne a little; but now, being bound to him by that unpleasantly significant legend, the tie chafed her sorely, and occasionally she had felt as though very little would turn the tide of her opinion, and make her dislike him intensely. She knew that she was never happier for his presence; she was even compelled to acknowledge the secret feeling that she was slightly relieved when circumstances interfered with his visits, and her own heart told her that she had never so nearly hated him as when he had pressed his first gracious bethrothal kiss upon her shrinking lips. She knew pretty girls who were engaged, who seemed to be wondrously happy, and whose bright eyes were all the brighter and more tender for their lover's gallant speeches. She had never blushed under Geoffrey Treherne's most flattering addresses — she had even felt very uneasy under them. But then it was as Blanche had said, too late, and she must even bear the uncomfortable cross with a good grace, since she herself had taken it up.

And then, after this, there was an unexpected arrival at the Priory, and this arrival was no less a person than Lady Laura's guardian, Mr. Jernyngham, who bore down upon his ward on his way to Scotland, with a characteristic weight of dignity, which almost overwhelmed that young lady. He was making a business tour, and his object in calling was to state his approval of the engagement, with, of course, a slight reservation in behalf of the magnificence of Basil de Tresham. The match was a fitting one in every point of view; but, of course, no honor could be done, and nothing could be added to the stately loftiness of the house of Tresham, despite the much-to-be-regretted fact that its sole present representative was merely a blue, velvet-eyed, golden-haired young lady, whose affairs of the heart were in an unpleasantly complicated state.

Under the heavy pressure of her guardian's presence, Laura felt her courage subsiding rapidly. What would he have said had he known with what an inward shrinking she received his graciously proffered congratulations in their first private interview? What would he have said, had he known what an unlady-like impulse directed her, after the interview was over, to snub her dignified bethrothed upon his arrival? What would he think if he knew that the lucky son of a "person in trade" carried her glove in his pocket, and monopolized her secret thoughts, to the great detriment of her affianced?

The new arrival patronized Robert Lindsay with great majesty, but not at all to the young man's confusion. He was becoming used to some degree of patronage, and could bear it with the most undiminished cheerfulness. He had even told Blanche Charnley that he rather liked it, to that young lady's intense amusement. Thus it may be easily seen, that the struggle going on was a very unequal one. Laura Tresham was easily influenced — Robert Lindsay scarcely to be influenced at all. During the two days of her guardian's stay, her fair young ladyship's patience was tried beyond all bounds. Treherne's eyes were gradually opening to a knowledge of the fact that his rival was more persevering than he had imagined. Circumstances, too, seemed to favor Rob Lindsay wondrously, in the face of his first want of success. He found himself unavoidably, as it appeared, thrown into Lady Laura's path. Perhaps diplomacy on Blanche's part assisted him. Blanche Charnley was a thorough feminine plotter, and worked with a will.

"She shall not marry Geoffrey Treherne if I can help it," she said, desperately; "and certainly she won't if Robert Lindsay can help it."

8

CHAPTER VIII.

"I CANNOT LISTEN TO YOU."

SO she managed to bring about interviews
that were absolutely unavoidable; so she
forbore to uphold her favorite, but let him uphold
himself; so she privately inquired into the facts
of his kindliness toward the little deformed
daughter of the under-gardener, and, dropping a
chance word here and there, aroused Laura's
secret sympathy, and that most powerful of all
feminine feelings, curiosity.

Then it was that Rob, for the first time, began
to recognize a faint shadow of sadness in the soft,
girlish eyes he loved so well, and for whose sake
he was doing such steadfast battle; and it ap-
pealed to his tenderness. A man with less hearty
strength of purpose would have long before
abandoned a struggle in which the odds seemed

so fearfully against him; but Rob Lindsay's belief in the simple strength of faith and endurance
was a very powerful one. Circumstances had
proved to him clearly that Laura Tresham's lover
was even a far less successful man than himself
in the matter of having won Laura Tresham's
heart. Was he sure that he had won Laura Tresham's heart himself? Well, of late he had even
dared sometimes to think so, and decidedly he
was not sure that he had not won it, which was
really some cause for rejoicing. Thus he did not
despair.

But, after her guardian's visit, Laura was rendered desperate. She was not safe after all;
she was even more unsafe than she had ever been
before; and thus, out of her desperation, there
grew a resolve almost as desperate as her first
one. She would speak to Mr. Lindsay openly;
she would force him to defend himself; she would
tell him that his absurd persistence was worse
than hopeless, and then, if this did not result in

his being utterly defeated, she would return to London. That would end the matter, surely. But she did not acknowledge to herself, even in her most secret thoughts, that London was her last, her very last resource, and that London, even though presenting itself as a haven of refuge from this too courageous lover, loomed up before her reluctant mental vision with bitter gloom.

Northumberland had been so pleasant, she said, inwardly; and it was because Northumberland had been so pleasant that she was so unwilling to leave it. But then she must go some day, and already she had far outstayed the usual term of her summer visits. She had been at the Priory nearly three months, and, notwithstanding her grievances, the three months had seemed terribly short. No opportunity for the consummation of her plans presented itself to her for several days. But, at length, one evening, as she came out of her room to go down to dinner, the door of

Robert Lindsay's room opened behind her, just as it had done on the evening of his arrival. On the impulse of the moment she spoke to him.

"She wished to speak to him alone," she said. "It was necessary that she should see him alone, because, what she was desirous of saying to him, could not be said in the presence of others."

Rob bowed composedly, but, nevertheless, with some surprise in his eyes. He would return to the dining-room, after dinner, at any time that would suit Lady Laura's plans.

Lady Laura's desperation was more intense than ever, and the embarrassed pink on her cheek burned into rose. Half an hour after dinner would do. This was all she had to say, and there she left him; and he discovered that he had taken his old stand again, unconsciously, and was watching the sweep of her rich dinner-dress, just as he had done once before.

And half an hour after the dinner was over, he sauntered back to the dining-room, and found her young ladyship awaiting him, and pretending to read by the light of the chandelier. But the reading was such a poor little pretence, that, in spite of her attempts to preserve a beautiful unconsciousness of the embarrassment of her position, she colored most transparently.

Rob took his stand complacently. He was rather curious to see how the matter would end; but, notwithstanding the faint inkling he had of its portent, he was not much discomposed. He was not the man to be discomposed by a pretty girl; and Lady Laura Tresham had never looked so pretty, so innocent, and so girlish, as she did just at the moment she closed her book, with the flicker of embarrassed light in her eyes.

Rob was quite conscious of her embarrassment, and very conscious indeed of the prettiness and girlish timidity of manner. Perhaps he had never admired Laura Tresham so much as he did that instant; and decidedly he had never felt so steady in his determination to do honest battle **for her sweet sake.**

It was at least five minutes before Lady Laura summoned a sufficient amount of courage to allow of her broaching the subject of her grievance, and when the courage was summoned, and the subject broached, it was done with some slight degree of tameness. She scarcely knew what she said as a beginning; but she was quite conscious that it was very weakly said, and that her knowledge of her weakness burned even her white forehead like fire. Altogether, her appeal was something like a sudden little burst of feeling, half like a small denunciation, half like a reluctant reproach; and it ended by accusing Robert Lindsay of being unjust and unkind.

"You made me appear absurd before," she said, "and you are making me appear absurd again; worse still, you are forcing me to make myself appear absurd."

"In whose eyes?" repeated Rob, just as he had done before. "Don't say in mine, Lady Laura."

She scarcely deigned to look at him. By the repetition of her grievances she had almost managed to make herself angry, and she felt it to her advantage to add as much fuel as possible to her wrath, lest it might come to a weak conclusion.

"It is ridiculous," she said, again. "You know it is, Mr. Lindsay. And if your intention was to make me feel wretched and uncomfortable, you have certainly been successful."

"I did not intend to make you uncomfortable," said Rob.

"If — if I were not — engaged," with a little dash at the last word, and a great dash of new color, "you know that you — that I — I mean to say — you know that you are treating me very unjustly, Mr. Lindsay."

She stopped here, petulant and excited, and waited for his reply, without looking at him. At this juncture Rob rose from his seat, and, slightly to her wonder, took two or three abrupt

turns across the room. Then he came back, and
folding his arms on the high back of his chair,
looked down at her bright, bent head, and petulant, fair face.

"Why, Lady Laura?" he asked.

Now this was really trying; and not only trying, but confusing. Necessarily the two or three
abrupt turns across the room had taken some
short time, and necessarily this lapse of time,
short as it was, had wholly unprepared Lady
Laura for this composed inquiry. In her surprise and embarrassment she forgot herself, and
looked up at him, and thus became more confused than ever.

"I really don't understand you, Mr. Lindsay,"
she said.

"Then I can easily make myself understood, I
suppose," answered Rob, cheerfully, "by speaking more plainly. Why is it absurd that I should
love you? Why is it absurd that I should wish
to tell you so? Why is it absurd that I should

wish to win you as Geoffrey Treherne did? That
is what I mean?"

Frank and fearless as he always was, and as
she had always known him to be, this was more
than she had expected. She had never thought
he would dare so far as this at least, and the
sudden knowledge that the worst had come to
the worst, indeed, was such a shock to her that
she felt powerless, and lost even the atom of self-
possession of which she might perhaps have
boasted a few minutes before. And, apart from
this, having admired him a little in secret, and
having been so often conquered by his fearlessness in their battles, there was something almost
touching in the fact of this fearlessness asserting
itself so strongly. And since she was thus
touched for the moment, there was no help for
her, for, be she as proud as she may, when a
woman is touched indeed, she is weaker than
even her worst enemies may fancy. She looked
up at him once, and faltered; she looked up at

him again, and felt his strength; she looked a third time, and acknowledged her own weakness, and remembering nothing but this weakness, got up from her chair, hurriedly, and broke down into a pretty, sudden appeal, that was wonderfully unexpected even to him.

"You ought not to say such things to me," she said, desperately. "You must know it is wrong, and — cruel. Ah, Mr. Lindsay! why wont you have pity on me, and be reasonable?"

From his place behind the chair, upon whose high back he leaned, Rob looked down at this fair, despairing enchantress, with a great deal of serenity of manner. He was not a Geoffrey Treherne, and his pride was not of the Treherne order, inasmuch as it had more of self-respect, and less of self-sufficiency about it. Laura Tresham could not overpower him with her stately coldness. She had struggled against him with her utmost power; she had called him awkward and presuming; she had sneered at him when

she spoke of him to Blanche Charnley; but she
had never daunted him in the least, and, in spite
of her sneers, she had not been able to resist him
in the end; and here she was sitting with him
alone, giving him, this big, underbred American,
an interview, in spite of herself, and feeling fully
conscious that she was getting the worst of the
combat.

Rob was cheerful, composed, serene, good-
humored to everything; and with his serenity
he baffled her once more, and scattered her self-
possession, and her self-possessed plans to the
winds.

"Reasonable!" he echoed, when she had
finished speaking. "Am I unreasonable, Lady
Laura? Is it unreasonable that I should love
you, and that loving you I should have determined to win you, if I might, in spite of the
world, in spite of Col. Treherne, in spite of William the Conqueror, who, it appears, has stood
between me and my man's right to say to you,

like an honorable gentleman, 'Laura, I love you. Give me the blessed right to call you wife.'"

She turned upon him, actually feeling pale, notwithstanding her poor little pretence of anger.

"You are going too far," she cried, more desperately than ever. "I cannot listen to you — I will not listen to you. I asked you to have pity on me, and you have no pity. I will not appeal to you again. You are unjust, and unkind, and wicked!" And she hid her face in her hands.

There was a short silence, not without its sting of bitterness to Rob, just the momentary sting he had felt so often before—a sting bitter enough though it passed away.

"Ah, Laura!" he said, at length, almost sadly, it seemed. "I cannot even ask you to forgive me; for what is there to forgive, and how can I regret that I have loved you? You are not Lord Tresham's daughter to me — you are only a woman, — the woman I love with all my soul, and all my strength; and since I am a man, I

have not feared your stately pride, for, by my
life, if love, and patient faith, and man's honor,
can win a woman, I will win you yet, in spite of
ten William the Conquerors. If you had loved
Geoffrey Treherne, or if, without having won
your love, he could make you happier than I
could, I would lay my love at your feet, and
leave you here with him, and go back to America
to-morrow. But you do not love him, and, in
your secret heart, you dread the marriage; and
if I can save you from it, I will not give you up.
I will not — I will not, by my faith."

Laura started from her seat again, white with
wrath and agitation, and the two faced each
other as they had never done before — their sudden mood a new one.

Rob stood up too, no longer leaning upon the
chair, but erect, and with his arms folded, his
careless good-humor overruled by something in
finitely deeper and more worthy—the something
innately natural to the man, but a something he
did not show every day.

"How dare you!" Laura flashed out. "How dare you say I do not love Col. Treherne? What right have you to presume to say so? You are insolent, indeed, sir."

Rob came nearer to her, with an odd, repressed fire in his steady, handsome eyes.

"Laura!" he said, with almost singular steadiness, "Say that you love him, and I will leave you now."

She opened her lips, looked at him, and stopped. She thought of Geoffrey Treherne, and his half-measured love; she thought of Lady Laura Treherne in the future, and turned paler than before. Rob Lindsay had conquered her again. But her anger and wounded pride came to her aid, and helped her, and she turned away, haughtily.

"I shall not say so," she said. "I shall not reply to a question so insolent. Your presumption is unpardonable!" And, having said this, she swept by, and left him standing in the middle of the room alone.

Then she went to her chamber, and wrote a letter to her guardian.

"I am going back to London with Mr. Jernyngham, when he returns," she said to Blanche, who found her in the middle of it. "I must go back, some time, you know, and I think I had better go now."

Nor could all Blanche's entreaties change the Lady Laura's determination.

CHAPTER IX.

"GOOD-BY, LADY LAURA."

IT is very probable that, after Lady Laura's departure, despite the muir-fowl and the tactful good-nature of the Charnleys, Northumberland seemed, for a day or so, a trifle dull to Rob Lindsay. There was a strange sense of lonely emptiness, even in the delightful, cozy, old-fashioned rooms of the Priory, since the sweet, proud face illumined them no longer. And, besides this, the autumn having fairly set in, had set in, of course, in good old dismal English fashion, with gray, leaden clouds, and drizzling, suicide-suggesting rains, and dropping, sodden leaves. It was a little disheartening, too, to hear, in the course of a week, that Treherne had run down to London; and it was equally disheartening to guess the cause of his visit; but still Rob

9

Lindsay did not quite lose courage. It would not do, however, to remain at the Priory very much longer; so, after a week's lounging, and reading, and grouse-shooting, he decided that he would continue his travels, as he had from the first intended doing; and, having come to this decision, he broached his plans to Ralph Charnley.

"You see," he said, "I promised myself a comfortable, careless, amateur sort of a tour through the Old World; and I am of the opinion that it would be all the pleasanter for a companion. Why can't you cram your things into a valise and come along with me?"

Ralph was highly pleased. There was nothing to prevent him doing so, he said.

"We will go wherever the guide-books tell us to go," said Rob, sagaciously; "and we will stay at each place until we want to go somewhere else. That's my mode of travel."

"It's a first-class one," answered Ralph, with an admiring glance at the strengthful, idle figure, stretched full length upon the sofa. "And we might stop in London a day or so, on our way."

"So we might," said Rob, as coolly as though the idea had just occurred to him.

"And we might call upon Jernyngham and see Lady Laura. Blanche had a letter from her this morning, and it appears she is not very well." This with great gravity of demeanor, but also with a side-glance, not unlike one of Blanche's, at the good-looking, brown-eyed face opposite.

The brown-eyed face had changed slightly, it seemed, for the instant; a flicker of light passed over it, touching the brown eyes with tenderness. Ah! Lady Laura, you were only a girl to him — a girl whom he loved, and for whom he had a sudden sense of pity, through his fancy of the imposing Chancery representative of Geoffrey Treherne combining themselves with the brazen weight of Basil de Tresham.

"Laura Tresham is a charming girl," Ralph remarked, casually, as it were; "but she has made a great mistake, in my opinion."

"How?" asked Rob, calmly and reflectively surveying the light wreaths of smoke curling up from the end of his cigar.

"How, indeed!" echoed young Charnley. "Just as a hundred other women do every day Treherne is a magnificent, gentlemanly idiot."

"Oh! you mean Treherne, do you?" Rob returned, still looking at his cigar wreaths. "Well, perhaps I am scarcely qualified to judge whether you are right or not, inasmuch as—" And here he stopped.

"Inasmuch as?" was Ralph's quiet suggestion.

Rob laughed.

"Inasmuch as," he answered, with considerable candor—"Yes; inasmuch as Treherne won where I lost—for the time being."

Ralph gave him another of the quick glances that were so like Blanche's.

"For the time being?" he repeated.

"Exactly," said Rob, good-humoredly. "'He

who fights and runs away, may live to fight
another day.'   And I did not run away, my dear
old fellow.   I was merely defeated, for the time
being, as I said before."

This was more than Ralph Charnley had expected to hear.   The fact was, he had been sym-
pathizing with his friend, to some extent, in
private.

"Does that mean you have not given her up
yet?" he asked, surprisedly.

"I don't give anything up easily," said Rob.
"I should not give a trifle up easily, and Laura
Tresham is not a trifle.   Yes, that is what it
means."

Ralph turned and looked at him from head to
foot—at his careless, handsome face, with its
heart of hidden strength; at his careless, handsome figure, carelessly expressing just the same
heart again; and having taken him in, as it were,
he shrugged his shoulders.

"You look as if you could turn the world,"

was his comprehensive comment; "and though you have before you the harder task of turning a woman, it suggests itself to me that there is not much doubt of your ultimate success."

"Thank you!" said Rob, succinctly.

A few days later, Lady Laura, sitting at. one of the iron-balconied windows of the Jernyngham mansion, was startled by the sight of a familiar, careless, well-knit figure, that was being ushered through the big entrance gates by the porter. Naturally she was startled, for she had imagined this same careless, well-knit figure to be at that moment looking out at the rain and mist, from certain windows in Northumberland.

She rose from her seat hurriedly, feeling not a little agitated. She must refuse to see him, of course. And then a sudden thought arose to her mind: he was going away! Perhaps he was going back to America, and they might not meet again! And he had not been so very wrong, after all. And — and — the truth was, she could

not quite make up her mind to dismiss this brave,
indefatigable suitor without a farewell word. A
moment more, and a card was handed to her by
a servant, who looked at her slightly agitated
face with something of wonder.

"Robert Lindsay."

She read it two or three times, to steady herself. Since it might be a farewell visit, perhaps
it would be better to see him — at any rate, it
would be the easier plan. Accordingly, she went
into the drawing-room, where Rob awaited her
arrival.

His stay was not a long one, however. He
was not going back to America, after all; and,
her fears on this point relieved, Laura could not
resist a very conscious remembrance of their
last interview. It was rather a difficult matter
to refer to the Charnleys, and the summer visit,
and still steer clear of the hidden quicksands,
and, in endeavoring to do so, she found herself
becoming entangled, as usual. She was wretch-

edly uneasy under his presence. She had been wretched ever since she had left Northumberland. She had been terribly wretched under the infliction of Geoffrey Treherne's visits; and Robert Lindsay's unexpected presence proved to her, before many minutes had passed, that the acme of her wretchedness was yet to be reached. It was useless to attempt to appear at ease. The slow, tell-tale fire crept up on her cheeks at his first glance, and in his brief stay it deepened and burned into a steady flame. He did not refer to the past at all during their interview, but when, at last, he rose to go, his careless mood seemed to change, and a momentary shadow of inward feeling fell upon him. He had tried in vain to rouse her to something of freedom and frankness, and his visible failure had stung him somewhat.

"When I was a boy at school," he said "they used to say I was a fortunate fellow, as a rule, and Lindsay's luck was a sort of proverb. But

it seems to have failed me a little at last. In an
hour from now, I dare say, I shall not feel that I
am battling against fate; but just now I do feel
it, strongly. Good-by, Lady Laura." And he
held out his hand.

She took it, feeling terribly at a loss for some
speech sufficiently cold and inapropos of the
subject.

"Will your absence be a long one?" she faltered, awkwardly.

He glanced down at her face, and then at the
hand he held — the hand with the legendary
Treherne diamond upon it.

"I scarcely know," he said. "It seems, just
now, you see, as if I were something like one
too many; but, when that feeling wears away, I
dare say you will see me again; and then perhaps it will be to hear me say, 'Good-by, Lady
Laura Treherne.'"

She stood behind the heavy curtains of the
window, and watched him pass out of the en-

trance-gate, just as she had watched him pass in, and, as the last echo of his footsteps sounded upon the wet pavement, she felt an odd, uncomfortable pressure on her throat — that uncomfortable, suffocating throb, which wet days and adverse tales bring to women, now and then, as a punishment for their small transgressions; then a hot drop slipped down her cheek and flashed upon her hand, very near the Treherne diamond; and then another and another, fast and heavily.

"It is the dull weather," she said — "the dull weather, and the loneliness, and — and everything. I wish I had never gone up to Northumberland I wish I was a beggar or a servant-maid. Ah! Blanche was right in saying that I had better have been anybody than Lady Laura Tresham."

CHAPTER X.

YES, OR NO?

A ND this was the beginning of a new era
of stronger dissatisfaction. If she had
scarcely cared for Geoffrey Treherne before, as
the slow, heavy winter months lagged by, she
almost hated him. Very naturally, Col. Treherne was becoming impatient. Of course, the
engagement must be consummated at some time;
and, in Col. Treherne's opinion, Lady Laura's
desire to delay this consummation was a very extraordinary one. He discussed the matter with
her guardian, and that gentleman bore down
upon his ward with a weight of argumentative
eloquence which added to her troubles in no in-
considerable manner. London had never seemed
to her so wearily, heavily dull, and the great
iron-balconied, iron-grated house, so intolerant in

its stubborn assertion of itself. That slowest and most dignified of carriages, adorned with Basil de Tresham's coat of arms, in bearing its fair freight and her card-case from house to house on occasional dismal mornings, might figuratively be said to have been driving her, not through her round of indispensable morning calls, but driving her to desperation. And, apart from all other adverse turns of fortune, really Lady Laura Tresham was not greatly to be envied, after all. With all the gloomy dignity of Basil de Tresham's line concentrated on her own girlish existence, with no home-ties, and few near friends, it is not to be wondered at that the bright home-comforts of the Priory seemed to her a haven of rest and delight. In those days, between her weariness and Geoffrey Treherne, she lost spirit and animation, and actually something of the delicate rose heart-coloring, formerly so charming. Now and then Blanche's letters brought tidings of the two travelers.

Ralph and Mr. Lindsay were in Naples. Ralph and Mr. Lindsay had been to Rome, and had picked up some pretty oddities in an antiquary's shop in some out-of-the-way place or other, and, having picked them up, had sent them home as presents.

"Mamma is more in love with Robert Lindsay than ever," the young lady wrote. "He has written to her once or twice, in that honest, hearty, boyish fashion of his, and she watches for his letters quite as anxiously as she does for Ralph's."

Now and then, too, there came whimsical scraps of news, that were plainly from this life-enjoying Rob Lindsay's pen; and these Lady Laura read oftener than all the rest. She fell into a fashion of sitting, with her hands folded upon her knee, before the fire, in her rich, desolate room, and slipping into sad, fanciful, girl-like reveries concerning this same Rob Lindsay. How would it have been, if he had been Geoffrey Treherne, or if she had not been so sternly set under the shadow of De Tresham's exclusive greatness? Would she have dreaded the letter-reading and the letter-writing, then? Would she have felt that dreadful impulse to be almost rude in her coldness, when she found herself alone with Col. Treherne, doomed to sustain with amiability her character of engaged young lady?

She never did more than ask herself these questions; but the time came when she knew she could have answered them with little trouble, and answered them truly, too.

But at length the time came also, when Geoffrey Treherne could be set aside no longer, and then her strait was a desperate one indeed. He came up to London, and had an interview with her guardian, which resulted as might have been expected. Through sheer force of superior power his point was gained, and the day fixed for the wedding. There was a rush and bustle

of trousseau-ordering, a steady, portentous driving of the stately carriage to jewelers and mil-
liners; and then, after each day, there came to
Laura Tresham, in her lonely, handsome chamber, more of the sad fireside reveries, and something very much stranger than even the old
impatience and dread.

In the letters that went from London to Northumberland, it is probable that something of the
unpleasant truth crept out. Of course, Lady
Laura did not say to her friend that she was a
very miserable young lady, and that she dreaded
the approaching marriage more intensely every
day. Of course she did not say, that in defiance
of her struggles, her heart was following with
the utmost impropriety, the gay tourist, who
seemed to be enjoying himself so vigorously;
and, of course, above all, she did not say that,
but for the fact that she was a very cowardly
young lady, she would have rid herself of the
legendary Treherne diamond, any day, for this

gay tourist's sake, and have been very heartily glad to do so. But, though she did not say this, her letters told Blanche Charnley that her fair friend was "lonely," and "blue," and "not very well;" that she found London insupportable, and had never enjoyed anything so much as that summer's visit. More, too, than this, they spoke with such evident shrinking of the arrangements made, and so slurred over all mention of the bridegroom, and so sadly touched, now and then, upon "helplessness" and "friendlessness," that Blanche arched her piquant eyebrows over them, and shrugged her piquant shoulders, and often ended with a little impatient " pah ! "

But at length an epistle came which broke through all restraint in a most unexpected manner. It was about three months before the day decided upon for the wedding that this letter arrived; and it was most unfeignedly tear blotted, and most unfeignedly wretched and despairing in tone. It was plainly a burst of appealing

desperation, the result of a sudden rush of hopeless misery, and it ended by imploring Blanche
to come to London at once.

Having read it, Blanche did not say "pah!"
she said, "Poor Laura!" and, after saying it, sat
down and wrote a reply, announcing her intention
of complying with the request. Then she re-
opened a letter she had just written to the tour-
ists, who for the past three weeks had been in
Paris, and, after inclosing a short note to Robert
Lindsay, sent it at once to Guestwick to be
mailed.

Two days after this, a carriage, containing
Miss Charnley and appurtenances, drew up before
the iron entrance-gates of Mr. Jernyngham's
town establishment; and the visitor, after having
been received with state and ceremony, was
delivered into the hands of her friend.

Not many minutes were required to show
Blanche Charnley exactly how affairs stood.
Laura looked pale and harassed. The last two

10

months had left their traces upon her so unmis-
takably, that, in the face of her impatience
Blanche felt constrained to pity her. But it was
not until late at night, when, having retired to
their room, they were safe from all chance of
disturbance, that she brought her energies to
bear openly upon the matter in hand. Then,
having settled herself, after her usual fashion,
for a comfortable "talk," she dashed at the subject.

"Now, Laura," she said, collectedly, "be good
enough to tell me all about it."

Thus taken by surprise, Lady Laura found her
color again, and then after twisting Geoffrey
Treherne's ring round her finger for one nervous
moment, lost it again, and was dumb.

"My dear child," persisted Blanche, after the
manner of the most elderly and experienced of
matrons. "My dear child, there is no earthly
use in pretending now, because it is very much
too late, and we are in far too critical a position;

so we may as well be perfectly frank and truth-
ful — as frank as Mr. Rob Lindsay would be himself, for instance."

But Laura, covered with convicted guiltiness,
did not speak, perhaps in consequence of having
most unaccountably found her color once more
at the last clause of the sentence.

"So, as we are to be frank," Blanche went on,
"I may as well begin by asking you a few frank
questions, which you are under obligations to
reply to frankly, however much they may startle
you. Will you answer them, Laura?"

"Yes," answered Laura, in the lowest of obe-
dient voices.

"Well," said her friend, "question first: Do
you want to marry Geoffrey Treherne?"

"N—o;" very low indeed.

Blanche nodded.

"I thought not," she said. "Miss Laura, no
weakness, if you please. Question second: Do
you want to marry Robert Lindsay?"

A little cowardly catch of Laura's breath, and then a decided dead silence.

"I will give you three chances, as the children do," said Blanche. "There, you weak-minded little creature." (With delightful inconsistency, inasmuch as Lady Laura Tresham was by no means a little creature.) "Once! Do you want to marry Robert Lindsay? Twice! Do you want to marry Robert Lindsay? Three times — "

"I — don't know!" broke in her victim. "Oh, Blanche, please don't!"

"You don't know?" echoed Blanche, indignantly. "Call yourself twenty years old, and don't know your own mind yet! Yes, you do know, and I know, too. You do want to marry Robert Lindsay, and you would marry him to-morrow, if you were not a miserable coward — afraid of Geoffrey Treherne, and afraid of Mr. Jernyngham, and afraid of every one else, who is kind enough to insist that you have not a will

of your own. Oh, you ridiculous little simple-
ton! How you do try my patience!"

In this manner, openly convicted of cowardice
and weakness, and all other capital crimes, the
fair culprit was completely subjugated, and very
naturally gave way, under the combined weight
of her misfortunes.

She was miserable, she said, in the greatest
depression. She was wretched. She did not
want to marry Geoffrey Treherne; but — but
how could she help herself. She wished she had
never gone to Northumberland!

Altogether, the scene, in its thorough girlish-
ness and incongruity of words, was not without
its whimsical side. In the short pause that followed this declaration, Blanche looked into the
fire, smiling, a little, notwithstanding her thought-
fulness.

"Laura," she said at last. "I have not yet
asked question third. When Robert Lindsay

comes to London — comes here — will you see him ?"

Laura looked up with a faint start.

"When — ?" she faltered.

"I said when," answered Blanche. "And I meant when. I have written to him, and told him to come."

CHAPTER XI.

THREE DAYS AGO!

CERTAINLY Blanche Charnley had her girlish hands full during the following week!
Perhaps no young lady in the world had ever felt
a greater consciousness of secret guilt than that
beautiful arrant coward, Lady Laura Treshar
and this consciousness by no means rendered
her the most animated of companions. She was
harassed and dejected, and even Blanche's most
spirited arguments failed to inspire her with anything of courage. Consequently Blanche waited
with some impatience for Robert Lindsay's
appearance. She had not decided as yet what
his appearance would bring forth, or what he
would do; but, having infinite faith in his powers,
she had at least decided that he would settle the
matter one way or the other.

"If I were in your place," she said, severely,
to Laura, when she had arrived at this decision,
"I would not wait for any one to settle my love
affairs for me. I would settle them myself. I
would write to Geoffrey Treherne, and tell him
that I *wouldn't* marry him. I should like to
know what calamity such a course would bring
forth. You are not a Circassian, I hope, or a
Turk, or a Chinese woman. If you are," with
excessive tartness, "I have not heard of it yet."

"I am not waiting for any one to settle my
love affairs," said Laura. "It is too late now,"
with a little sigh.

Blanche shrugged her shoulders, satirically.

"Too late!" she began. "Robert Lindsay—'

Lady Laura rose from her chair, pale-faced and
subjugated, and walked to the window.

"Don't, Blanche!" she exclaimed. "Don't
talk to me about Robert Lindsay. It is too late,
and I am miserable enough." And she had
scarcely uttered the words, before she turned

paler still, and started from the window, crying out, suddenly, "Oh, Blanche, there he is!"

Blanche flung down her book, and hurried to the window, and to her excitement and delight, her first glance fell upon the careless, stalwart figure, which had so often been the object of her good-natured admiration — the figure of Robert Lindsay in person.

Laura drew back, excited, and nervous.

"I — I can't see him," she cried. "I — I really can't! What shall I do?"

Blanche fired in an instant like some small order of domestic fire-work. If she was to defeat Geoffrey Treherne, she must defeat him now; if she was to help this indefatigable, tender-hearted Rob, she must help him now; if she was to save Lady Laura from a life of half-love and slow disappointment, she must save her from it this very instant.

"You cannot see him!" she exclaimed. "Say you have not the courage to see him, and you will be right once; say you are weak-minded enough to be wicked, and you will be right again. You have been weak enough to treat Geoffrey Treherne shamefully, (not that he doesn't deserve it, because he does;) but you have still treated him shamefully, and now you are too weak to right him, and right yourself, and right the man who loves you, and who is worth five hundred thousand Geoffrey Trehernes. You won't see him?" with terrible calmness. "Very well, don't see him, and I will go back to Northumberland before breakfast to-morrow morning, and you can marry Geoffrey Treherne, and be wretched for life."

Lady Laura put both her hands up to her face, and covered it, her cheeks burning, her brow burning, the very tips of her ears burning; her heart beating so loudly that she was sure the room echoed with it.

Blanche drew from her trim little belt a trim little jewel of a watch.

"I will give you two minutes to decide," she said, emphatically. "The footman will be here in three, and if, by that time, you have not spoken, I shall ring for your maid to pack my trunks."

The first minute had passed, and the second was half gone, when Laura lifted her face, and broke the ominous silence.

"I — I will see him," she faltered.

Blanche shut her watch with a little click, just as the servant opened the door.

"Show the gentleman into this room, Martin," she said; and, as the man withdrew, she turned to Laura. "I shall stay in the room long enough to speak a dozen words to Mr. Lindsay, and then I shall go down stairs," she said. "Laura, you have no need to be afraid that you are not ready to meet him. Your cheeks are on fire, and you look like an angel. There, my dear, be sensible, and think what Lady Laura Treherne would be twenty years hence."

Laura had no time to speak. Her breath was fairly taken by this master-stroke of rapidity and diplomatic movement. The fact was, that if she had had time to speak, or even to think, she would have been so full of misgiving that she would have upset the best laid plans in the universe, and of this Blanche Charnley was very well aware. But, with the shock of Blanche's sudden indignation, and that last stroke concerning Lady Laura Treherne's future, accumulating at once, she found herself absolutely free to let things take their own course.

She did not know how much Blanche had written to Robert Lindsay; she had not even dared to guess heretofore; but when the two met, a full recognition of the truth flashed upon her.

"I am not going to ask you any question now," said Blanche, after the first greetings had been exchanged. "I am going to leave you to say what you have to say to Laura. Mr. Lindsay, two weeks ago, the young lady told me that she was wretched and despairing, and guess why! Because, if she is not saved from it, in less than three months from now, she is to marry Geoffrey Treherne. Once you told me that if you could save her from it, you would; and so, as there was no time to lose I sent for you. Save her if you can."

Lady Laura did not look at her visitor when Blanche's exit left them alone. She dared not even glance up, but waited in silence, her burning blushes almost stinging her delicate skin. She was thinking that this was worse than all the rest. Rob Lindsay was thinking that this was his last chance, and that there would be a hard struggle, before he would let it slip away from him, and be lost.

"You see that I have come back again, Lady Laura," were his first words. "And I think there is no need of telling you why I came."

"Excuse my saying so —" she said, trying to appear cold, and quite conscious that she appeared nervous.   "But I really don't know why, Mr. Lindsay."

"Then I suppose I must even tell you again," Rob replied quietly.   "The reason is an old one, Lady Laura, and one I have given more than once before.   It is a simple one, too.   I came back because I love you."

She was conscious of a sudden throb of the smoothly-beating heart that Geoffrey Treherne's warmest words had never had the power to stir. She was conscious, too, of a quicker pulse-beating, and an odd, exultant thrill ruling her in spite of her confusion.   He had not given her up after all.   He loved her yet.

"Do you understand me?" he said again.   "I think you do, and I will tell you something else, Lady Laura.   I think if Col. Treherne were here, he would understand too, for he is an honorable man, at least; and I think sometimes that the worst of men are more merciful than the best of women.   I told you I loved you when we were in Northumberland, and I said I would not give you up; and I have not given you up yet."

There was a slight pause before the last word, and a slight stress upon it, when it was uttered, that Laura Tresham's heart beat hard.

She could see there was more steadiness in his manner than there had ever been before, and she fancied there was more bitterness, for, though he had not wholly flung aside his careless, good-humored audacity, he stood before her a man who felt that to some extent he had been wronged, and who was now throwing his last stake

"But I have not come back to ask you to pity me," he went on. "Perhaps sentiment is not my forte; at any rate, it seems that I am always oddly at a loss for fair speeches. I have not come to say that my heart will be broken, if, three months hence, Laura Tresham is lost to me forever in Lady Laura Treherne. Hearts are not easily broken in the nineteenth century. I will not even say my life would be blighted; but this I will say, Lady Laura Tresham, simply and honestly, I have loved you — I do love you; and the true woman who hears such words from the lips of a gentleman, will understand, simply and honestly, all that they mean.   The last time," he went on, "that we were alone together at the Priory, I said to you that if you would tell me that you loved Geoffrey Treherne, I would leave you at once.   You dared not tell me so, and yet Geoffrey Treherne's ring is on your finger now, and you are almost his wife.   Is that quite fair to Col. Treherne, Lady Laura?   Asking pardon for the apparent irreverence of the remark, is it exactly what Basil de Tresham (whose patrician blood is supposed to be as honorable as it is blue) would be likely to countenance?"

"I wish Basil de Tresham — " Lady Laura was beginning, disrespectfully, when she recollected herself and stopped.   In her desperation she had almost been sacrilegious.

"If you were going to say that you wished Basil de Tresham had never been born," said Rob, sagaciously, "I am compelled to say that my wishes coincide with yours most heartily. I am inclined to think that, perhaps, it would have been as well. Ah, Laura! but for Basil de Tresham, my love would not have been an audacity, and Geoffrey Treherne's success his birthright."

But the next moment his mood changed. She was only a girl, and she had made a mistake, and her rashness had brought to her its own retributive pangs, and the reproach in his tone forced them to reveal themselves. Rob forgot his satire and his bitterness. He crossed the hearth, and stood before her an instant, the full strength of a man's chivalrous love warming him, and stirring him to his heart's core.

"Lady Laura," he said, "there are tears in your eyes;" and then in a breath's space he was down upon one knee by her chair, with his arm around her waist.

11

"Laura," he said, "I *will* not lose you. If I have seemed bitter and careless, it was because I have suffered. I *cannot* lose you, I say again. I love you, and I will not let you go. It is not too late yet. I do not ask you to say that you love me. I only ask you to give the Treherne diamond back to its owner, and free yourself from this miserable engagement. I can wait for the rest. I will wait for the rest, patiently, until you choose to say to me that my probation is ended."

There were tears in her eyes — tears heavy and large, and, before he had finished speaking, they were dropping fast. Laura Tresham had not been made for a heroine; and her intention to immolate herself upon the altar of her ancestral greatness had resulted in too much of real martyrdom. It had not been easy, at first, to determine to give up this earnest, untiring lover for Geoffrey Treherne; but now it would cost her a struggle too great to be borne. Her own

natural weakness was quite as much in favor of
the earnestness and untiring zeal, as if she had
been fortunate enough to be a young lady of far
less patrician antecedents. With her trouble
and excitement, and with Rob Lindsay's strong,
persuasive arm around her waist, dignity, even
self-control was out of the question; and so she
dropped her beautiful face upon his shoulder.

"But—it—it is too late," she faltered, trembling
like a lovely coward as she was. "Oh,
Robert (with a little catch of the breath at her
own temerity), what could I say — to Colonel
Treherne?"

"Say?" echoed Rob, in a glow of enthusiastic
fire. "Say to him what I should wish a woman
to say to me, if she had bound herself to me
rashly. Say to him 'I have done you a wrong;
and, by marrying you, I should make it a crime.
I do not love you, and time has proved to me
that I was mistaken in fancying that I could;
and I appeal to you, as an honorable gentleman,

to release me from my promise.' It might not be easy to say, Laura, but, by saying it, you could save yourself from dishonor and wretchedness "

It is unnecessary to record all the circumstances connected with the remainder of the interview. Suffice it to say that, having love, and tears, and vanquished pride all on his side, Robert Lindsay gained the victory which was to bring to a conclusion his daring campaign, and that, upon his departure, Lady Laura had gained courage almost marvelously.

She went up stairs to Blanche Charnley all a-bloom with blush roses. Blanche had been awaiting her return with some impatience and a little fear, notwithstanding her faith in Rob; but, when she saw her, she experienced an immediate sense of relief.

"Well," she said, "does Mr. Lindsay leave England?"

Lady Laura slipped into a chair, with a soft,

expressive little sigh, and an equally expressive little deprecating smile.

"No —" she hesitated. "At least, I don't think so. I — am going to write a letter to Col. Treherne."

"Then you had better write it at once," advised Blanche, "before your courage oozes out of your finger ends, as usual, my dear."

"It — is written already," confessed her young ladyship, with considerable confusion of manner. "I — The fact is, Blanche, I wrote it two or three days ago; but — you see I was — I did not like to seal it — then."

Blanche sprang up from her chair, her amusement and exultation getting the better of her, at this guilelessly significant acknowledgment.

"Oh, ye daughters of men!" she exclaimed, laughing until the tears started to her eyes. "Oh, fairest and most courageous of the descendants of De Tresham! and you did not know whether you wanted to marry Robert Lindsay or not!"

"I have not said that I wanted to marry him, yet," said her ladyship, blushing more than ever. "He — has not even asked me if I would."

"Of course not," said Blanche. "And of course he does not know what you would say, if he did. Oh, Laura, Laura! and you wrote it two or three days ago!"

CHAPTER XII.

LUCK TURNS.

TO attempt to describe Col. Treherne's astonishment, when he fully comprehended the
turn affairs had taken, would be to openly dis-
play a weakness. It would not have been like
Geoffrey Treherne to expect effusion; and so, in
the earlier stages of the engagement, to his lim-
ited mental vision the coldness and brevity of the
letters of his affianced had simply implied a
becoming dignity and reserve; and thus, as he
had placidly read them in Northumberland, he
had been placidly unconscious of how fate was
working against him in London. But there was
a limit to even Geoffrey Treherne's shortsighted-
ness; and as the epistles became shorter and
more significantly cold, he had gradually awa-
kened to some slight sense of doubt: but still he
had not dreamed of such a finale to his dignified

love story as this. To be worsted in such a combat, at such a time, was bad enough; but to be worsted as he guessed he had been, was a terrible blow to his arrogant pride. And it must be confessed, my dear reader, that this fair descendant of De Tresham had acted with less of stoical dignity than had been customary with the dames of her noble house. It is quite probable that, a century or so ago, the fair De Tresham, who indiscreetly sacrificed herself, in a rash moment, to the family heroics, would have magnanimously and magnificently adhered to her resolution, even to the wreck of her life's happiness and her true lover's hope; which, no doubt, would have been very brave, and very honorable, and very worthy her illustrious name. But, as you have of course observed, this story of mine is not a tragedy, or its heroine a goddess. She is simply a young lady of the nineteenth century, with all the nineteenth-century weakness and faults; and, having made a very foolish mistake, and repented it, her lack of heroic determination is

neither her fault nor mine, but probably the
fault of the nineteenth century, which philoso-
phers assure us is a period terribly retrograded
from ancient Spartan virtue.

Summoned by Lady Laura's letter, Geoffrey
Treherne came to London at once; and then,
but for Blanche's presence and encouragement,
Laura's position, between her guardian's indignation and her ex-lover's somewhat haughty dis-
pleasure, would have completely overwhelmed
her. As it was, it was by no means a pleasant
one, and the termination of the interview between
the three tried all her resolution; but in the end,
of course, the majority on the side of love, carried the day; and, for perhaps the first time in
her wardship, the young lady withstood the
opposing power of her guardian's eloquence.
To that stately and somewhat pompous individual, his ward's unexpected firmness was almost
as astounding as her unprecedented offence. He
could not understand it, and was forced to retire
from the scene a vanquished potentate, and let

Treherne go back to Northumberland with the
legendary diamond in his portmanteau.

And then, very naturally, as a consequence of
the excitement, after the interview was brought
to a close, Laura's spirits flagged again, and she
was a very dejected young lady indeed. She
could not see Robert Lindsay now — she was not
sure that she wanted to see him at all, at first;
but, on finding that, for several days, Robert
Lindsay did not trouble her, her opinions began
gradually to change. The fact was, that Robert
Lindsay was a sagacious young man, and his
experience had taught him exactly what the
result of Treherne's visit would be; so, for a day
or so, he confined himself to occasional evening
strolls past the iron-balconied mansion; and it
was not until the end of the week that he entered
the iron gates.

The footman who opened the door, knew him
as a friend of Miss Charnley's; and when Rob
informed him, coolly, that there was no necessity
for his being announced, adding the pardonable

fiction that he was expected, he showed him, without further ceremony, into the room where the two young ladies were sitting.

Blanche greeted him delightedly. She was tired of waiting for a finale, and was getting out of patience. She had been expecting him, too, and Laura had not; consequently, Laura rose to meet him flushing and paling like the loveliest of grown-up children.

Before half an hour had passed, Blanche discreetly retired to the window with her work, and, taking a seat behind the curtains, counted her stitches as though her life depended upon the completion of every rose-bud she worked.

Lady Laura stood upon the hearth-rug in silence, her eyes fixed upon the fire, and, for a few moments after Blanche's discreet move, there was a slight lull in the conversation.

To Rob, Lady Laura Tresham had never seemed less Lady Laura Tresham, and more the woman he loved, than she did then. The blaze of the fire, dancing upon the white hand hanging idly

by her side, showed it the fairest of hand⸱ ⸱⸱
smooth, round wrist, set in a ruffle of web-like
lace, but showed no Treherne - diamond on the
slim forefinger; and so, not being the man to
brook delay, he went to her side and took it, this
passive white hand, in his.

"So long as you wore Treherne's ring," he
said, tenderly, "I only said I loved you, asking
for nothing; but, since I knew that you no
longer wore it, I have only waited, what I thought
would be your pleasure, to come to you, to speak
once again. Laura, you know what I am asking
you for?"

But Laura, fair traitress, said nothing.

But Rob was a frank wooer, and cared little
for her silence, since he knew what a sweet
truth it told; and he slipped his strong arm about
her slender waist, and drew her to his side, and
kissed her, as Geoffrey Treherne would never
have done, if he had loved her a thousand years.

"I said I would wait patiently," he said, kissing her hand. too. and then holding it to his

breast as he·spoke; "and so I have waited, Laura, nearly six days. And six days are six ages to a lover — a lover like me, dearest. And now I have come to you; and as I hold you in my arm, though you have not spoken a word to me, I can read in your sweet face that I am not to be wretched; and, before Heaven, my darling, I am a happy man."

But Laura, fair hypocrite, said nothing.

"See!" he said, drawing a little case from his pocket, and taking from it a sparkling, flashing ring, sapphire set. "See, Laura! no Norman brought this, to be handed down, with its legend, through generations of noble brides; no barons have worn it, and no kings have praised it; but I, Rob Lindsay, who love you with my whole soul, and my whole strength, and will love you through life and death, with a gentleman's faith and reverence, ask you to answer my appeal by letting me place it upon your hand, and, by wearing it there, until you give me the right to claim you for my wife."

And Laura, fair queen dethroned, and woman crowned, held out her white hand, the pure heart touched — pearl tears slipping softly away from her lashes for very joy.

Rob put it on, the sapphire-set circlet, and then caught her in both his strong arms, and kissed her again and again, until her blushes had almost dried her tears; and between tears and blushes she was fairer and fresher than ever.

Then, with his arm still round her waist, Rob took her to Blanche's window.

"Tell her, Laura, my dear!" he said, with a touch of his old, cheerful audacity.

Lady Laura laid the hand, wearing the sapphire ring, upon Blanche's shoulder.

"Blanche, dear," she said, with her most guilty, and, at the same time, most lovely hesitation, "I am — engaged to Mr. Lindsay."

Blanche rose with a little, happy ghost of a laugh; and then, of course, girl-like, broke off with a little, happy ghost of a sob; and then, taking refuge in the fair face, kissed it to the full as heartily as Rob had done.

"You see, Laura," she said to her friend that night, when they were alone, "You see, my dear, how exactly we grown-up children are like the children in story-books, and how much happier we are when we have been honest, and told the truth. Just imagine how wretched you would have been if you had not told the truth to Geoffrey Treherne and Robert Lindsay."

Very deeply struck by this philosophical application of a popular and much-preached conclusion, Lady Laura glanced down at her sapphire ring, which was sparkling beautifully in the fire light, and drew a soft, little sigh.

"Yes, dear," she said.

"And," began Blanche again. "Now, confess, Laura, now that the trouble is over, are you not just as glad as the story-book children are when they have spoken the truth, and have just found out how dreadfully they would have been punished if they hadn't?"

And the answer was another,

" Yes, dear."

The world frequently hears it said that Laura Lindsay is one of the happiest, and beautiful young matrons in the shire in her husband has settled down, and boug estate.   People say, too, that Mr. Lindsay of the most popular of men.   The countr try, whose pedigrees date back through cer of nobility and grandeur, respect and ι him.   He is popular because he is ger daring, and thoroughbred.   He leads men rank might entitle them to lead him ; and men are his best and nearest friends.   T astonishing luck, they say, in this man, w gained everything that fair fortune could ι

But Lady Laura, in whose wifely e; is, of course, a nineteenth century her that her husband's luck is simply her hu generosity, kindness, and courage.

THE END.

Printed in the United States
98329LV00017B/139/A